The Right to a Full Life

Dorothy E. B. Fickenscher

The Right to a Full Life
Copyright © 2023 by Dorothy E. B. Fickenscher

ISBN: 978-1639456185 (sc)
ISBN: 978-1639456192 (e)

Library of Congress Control Number: 2023908223

1All rights reserved. No part of this publication may be reproduced, distributed, or transmitted in any form or by any means, including photocopying, recording, or other electronic or mechanical methods, without the prior written permission of the publisher, except in the case brief quotations embodied in critical reviews and other noncommercial uses permitted by copyright law.

The views expressed in this book are solely those of the author and do not necessarily reflect the views of the publisher, and the publisher hereby disclaims any responsibility for them.

Writers' Branding
(877) 608-6550
www.writersbranding.com
media@writersbranding.com

Contents

Baby Steps 1
Becoming a Parent 5
Improvements in the Process 8
Becoming Courageous 9
The Early Years With Elaine 10
Parenting Twins 12
Turning a Neighborhood Into a Community 15
The Medical World and a Child With a Developmental Delay 18
The Good Patient 28
Dentists 29
The Medical World and Louis 30
Schools 32
Welcomed and Included 37
Life After High School 44
Perspective 47
Support Groups 49
Head of Household 52
Dreams 54
Church 56
Facing Crises 58
Fairness 61
Parenting Louis 62
An Individual First, not a Disability 68
A Work in Progress 70
Stubbornness or Persistence? 73
Sense of Time 74
Mood Shifting 75
Secrets 76

Social IQ	77
Dating and Marriage	80
Conceptualization and Anticipation	81
Self-Talk	83
Make Believe	84
Being Independent Versus Being Responsible	86
Self-Confidence	87
Exercise and Sports	88
A Picture is Worth a Thousand Words	90
Understanding and Being Understood.	92
Pronunciation or Communication?	94
Technological Aids to Communication	96
Truthfulness	98
Hygiene	99
Adjustments	101
Community	102
Why Would Anyone Wish to Curtail That?	104
Low Functioning or few Skills?	107
Moving Into a Place of One's Own	110
Out and About in the Community	112
Travel	115
Managing a Life	116
The Sandwich Generation	117
A Full Life	119
A Matter of Perspective	122

BABY STEPS

There was a knock on the door. Elaine got up from the chair, walked to the door, and opened it. "Come in, come in!" she said.

Two young men shook her hand, introduced themselves, and entered her apartment.

Almost immediately, they were sitting beside Elaine on the couch with a photo album open as Elaine pointed to pictures and talked about each one. She was totally engaged and soon they were as well.

Both men were students at the Uniformed Services University of Health Sciences in Bethesda, Maryland. As part of a class requirement, they must visit the home of a family with a family member with special needs. In this instance, the students were visiting the Germantown, Maryland, apartment of a young adult with Down syndrome. Elaine's roommate, an individual without disabilities, was still at work. Later her twin brother, Louis, will stop by on his way home from his job. He has Tourette's syndrome, but manages his tics well. Both Elaine and her brother will talk about their lives, what they want doctors to know, and then each will defer them to me, their mother, to help provide information about the medical challenges they faced earlier in their lives.

In 1984 ago I gave birth to these two. Elaine's diagnosis of Down syndrome was devastating, and at the time I never imagined that Elaine would develop the skills and confidence to live in her own place. I never imagined the full life she would have, nor did I envision the importance of surrounding her with a supportive and caring community. Even though my son has significant challenges, I always believed he could make it in the world on his own terms. The fact that both are making their way in life on their own terms is wonderful.

I have learned a great deal raising my children. The friendships developed with others within the special-needs community have enriched my life, and I have learned that I am stronger and more resourceful than I imagined. I set out to write about one hundred things I learned about individuals with Down syndrome. But my effort evolved into a more personal account of the lessons I learned while raising both children. Perhaps the biggest challenge in raising my daughter was to raise my own expectations initially and then raise the expectations of others about what she could do, because she has the facial features of someone with Down syndrome and has always looked different. My son, on the other hand, didn't and still does not look like he has a disability, and for him the challenge was getting the accommodations he needed so that he could develop to his potential.

What have I learned parenting these children while living out my own dreams? I have met and become friends with people I never would have had the opportunity to know, except that they, too, have children with special needs. I have learned that people with special needs have much to offer others, and so do I. I have no idea what life would have been like for me without Elaine and Louis, but I do know that many of the things I count as blessings are because, not in spite, of them.

I was born at the end of World War II into a loving family. My father had his own business. My mother, who stayed at home, was an unpaid partner in the family business, and in all ways made the family work. I have an older brother and two sisters. I was the second child, the first girl. As the first girl, I was named after both grandmothers – Dorothy Elaine. My family name was Buchanan, so my initials D.E.B. meant that a nickname for me was Debbie. In elementary school I preferred Dorothy, but when I attended a private school and nicknames were not allowed, I decided I liked to be called Debbie.

My mother had four children in five years. Being so close in age, at times we were the best of friends, and at other times we bickered heatedly. Breakfast and dinner were family times. We took vacations together. Family came first—always. Now that we are all adults, each of us has created a family with strong family ties. Everyone shows up for weddings and other family events. There is no such thing as a small event when our family gathers.

My parents encouraged each of us to develop as individuals. Education was important and my parents made sure each of us had a college education. I have a graduate degree plus did extensive postgraduate work. My liberal arts education helped me understand how to learn and how to problem solve, skills I have found incredibly useful in parenting and advocating for my children.

Although I wanted to have lots of children, I married late and found that it wasn't easy to get pregnant. When I did have children, I had twins—something no one else in the family had experienced, just as no one had experience with children with special needs. As a result, no one doled out advice and no one second-guessed me until my children reached their late teens. Then the differences of opinion stemmed more from my vision that each child would be as independent and as fully included in the community as possible and their vision that Elaine would be in a group home or possibly a "ranch" where those with disabilities work, live and socialize in a community of people with disabilities. After much discussion my siblings have come to understand that my vision for Elaine can be a reality.

After college I worked a few years in Europe. When I returned to the United States, I first settled in Boston, Massachusetts where I found a job as a secretary at a radio station and then a job working as a secretary at Harvard University. As I had always wanted to teach, I applied to the Master of Arts in Teaching program at Brown University within two years of my return to the United States. After I earned my M.A.T. I became a teacher in the public schools in Montgomery County, Maryland. My education and the skills I learned in the classroom helped prepare me for handling the various challenges that I encountered as a parent of first one and then two children with special needs. The children were born at the old Walter Reed Hospital in Washington, DC. At the time of their births, we lived in a neighborhood in the nation's capital. My daughter's diagnosis of Trisomy 21 (Down syndrome) was confirmed at her two-week checkup, but my son was not diagnosed with Attention Deficit Disorder until he was six years old, shortly after we moved to St. Louis, Missouri. The true diagnosis of Tourette's syndrome came at age nine, two years after we had relocated to Germantown, Maryland. By the time the children entered first grade, I was divorced and living on the East Coast while their father lived in the Midwest. I decided to keep my married name, Fickenscher, because I believed that it would be less confusing for Louis and Elaine if we all shared the same last name.

BECOMING A PARENT

The same day I learned I was having twins, I received a phone call from the social worker at the adoption agency we were using, notifying me that my husband and I had cleared the final hurtle toward adoption. Without a second thought, I stopped the adoption process and focused on the twins I was carrying.

For the next six months I read all I could about parenting twins because I thought that having twins was the main challenge I faced. As I was an elderly primagravida, the doctors informed me that I would be put on bed rest around the fifth month to prevent preeclampsia, a condition often associated with multiple births at my advanced age. I followed the doctors' orders, went on maternity leave, and took to my bed. Within weeks of bed rest at home, I was hospitalized due to concerns that one of the twins might die in utero. I lay in bed in a ward in a local military hospital for just under three months. Three weeks before my thirty-ninth birthday, the doctors decided to induce labor. Twelve hours after labor started, my daughter was born and my son arrived twenty minutes after that. Both babies were healthy and approximately the same length and weight. We were so relieved!

After the births I was initially moved to a private room rather than to a ward, which would have been the normal sequence of events. The obstetrician who had monitored my pregnancy wanted to discuss concerns about our daughter. The doctor said that there were indications that she had Down syndrome. A sample of her blood had been sent to the lab for a chromosome test. He told us that we would have the definitive answer at her two-week checkup. We were concerned, but mostly thrilled that both babies were healthy. We decided to keep the doctor's concerns about Elaine to ourselves when we announced the births.

After this discussion in the private room, I was moved into a room with four beds separated from each other by curtains. I was the only occupant. My husband left and I fell asleep. In the middle of the night the lights were turned on and another woman was moved to the bed next to mine. She settled in, and things quieted down. We were both asleep when the lights in the room were again turned on, and doctors surrounded her bed and woke her up. They told her that her baby was a mongoloid. She began sobbing. As she cried out for her husband, the doctors assured her that she was handling the news well. They said another woman had given birth earlier in the evening to twins and one also was a mongoloid. They told the sobbing woman that the other mother was in denial. The doctors eventually left, the lights were turned off, and I lay in bed sick at heart. I knew I was the one to whom they referred.

When I spoke to my husband the next morning (in those days the bedside phone was connected to a switchboard that was off at night), he reminded me that we were told to wait for the results of the chromosome test. We decided to do just that. Meanwhile, family and friends rejoiced at the healthy, if premature, arrival of our babies. Gifts, cards, and well-wishes poured in. Their births were celebrated.

When we arrived at the clinic for our second-week checkup, we were totally unprepared for the first words out of the pediatrician's mouth, "I will see the mongoloid first." My husband was angry and told the doctor he was talking about our child and this was not a term to be used. I cried. In fact, I was pretty close to tears for months. The prognosis was devastating. The pediatrician told us that at age seven Elaine would stop learning, and that what we did during her early years would make a huge difference. No one suggested institutionalization, but a very bleak picture of her future was all they could offer.

. . . .

After this appointment we went, as planned, to my parents' home for dinner. I was in tears as we shared the news that Elaine had Down syndrome. My father's immediate response was that he was willing to fix it, no matter the cost. We had to tell him that the extra chromosome was in every cell in her body. The best we could do was to do as much as possible in the first years of her life.

As a family we took this advice to heart and identified what we could do for, and with, Elaine in those first months of life. It certainly motivated us to read, ask, and learn as much as possible.

IMPROVEMENTS IN THE PROCESS

The military now has a program that goes a long way toward preventing such insensitivity and ignorance. Students at the Unified Services University of Health Sciences must take a class where they learn about children with special needs. The class involves home visits by students and a classroom session with roundtable discussions with parents about issues related to parenting children with special needs. The students who visit our family are amazed about the richness of my daughter's life. They enjoy asking my son about being a sibling of someone with developmental delays and engage in lengthy discussions with him about Tourette's syndrome.

Many of the students are training to be pediatricians. I believe the visits help them to understand the possibilities of enjoying a rich life in spite of a diagnosis of a significant disability. We like giving them tips on how to work with families like ours.

BECOMING COURAGEOUS

Before I had children, I avoided confrontation. I might inwardly steam, but I would literally walk around the block rather than confront anyone. However, my children needed an advocate, and I developed a backbone. Long before I learned how to advocate for myself, I learned how to stand up for my children. I think this is known as the Mama Bear response.

Being an advocate when the children were infants involved asking a lot of questions to make certain I understood the doctor's instructions. Then as Elaine began seeing specialists and therapists, I was the person who not only kept track of what happened at each appointment, I also was the one who shared what the other specialists were saying about, and prescribing for, Elaine. In essence, I was her caseworker. I kept a spiral notebook with a brief summary of each visit with a doctor or a therapist. This record keeping is now a routine at our HMO, but at the time the notebook definitely helped me. One time, the notebook helped shift the discussion when the professional seeing my daughter told me that my account of an earlier visit could not possibly be correct. I just handed over the notebook and the tone of our conversation shifted.

THE EARLY YEARS WITH ELAINE

In the beginning, we privately paid for speech and physical therapy for Elaine. The therapists worked with Elaine and taught me strategies to use with her. Because Elaine had such poor muscle tone, I learned how to hold her to stabilize her neck and then to help strengthen her neck muscles. She had to be positioned so that she was upright once she was big enough to sit. This was important so she would learn the proper position for eating. We learned how to help Elaine pronounce simple words, and early on we acquired a communication board with pictures so she could associate words with pictures and use the board to communicate. Things that Louis just picked up by observing others had to be broken down into manageable steps and taught to Elaine. The therapists who worked with her were at opposite ends of our metro area, so that involved a lot of driving in the morning traffic. It was a blessing that I worked only part of the day, teaching from late morning to mid-afternoon.

I do not know what I might have done if I had known during my pregnancy that one of the twins had an extra chromosome. We chose not to have amniocentesis because we understood the test might put both of the fetuses in jeopardy. While at the time, I did not think I could handle a child with disabilities, I did not want to put either fetus at risk. Later, I learned that there is a waiting list to adopt children with Down syndrome, but we never considered putting Elaine up for adoption. She was ours.

Sometime during that first month, a social worker told me that of all the things that could be wrong with an infant, Down syndrome was the best. She said that the more we did for, and with, Elaine, the more she would be able to do. That was a message of hope and it helped me focus. One of my sisters told me that although it was tragic that Elaine had Down syndrome, that Elaine was not a tragedy. Family and friends were sorry about the diagnosis of Trisomy 21, but they had met Elaine and as far as they were concerned, she was family.

While still on maternity/child-care leave, I tried to read everything I could get my hands on about Down syndrome. I worried that my daughter might never sit up or walk on her own.

Social workers took me to visit programs for toddlers with disabilities, to help me understand how much children with developmental delays can do, but I am sorry to admit that I saw only disabilities and not capabilities. I did not enjoy visiting the programs and convinced myself that my daughter did not belong in a program with disabled children. I failed to see the possibilities for my daughter. I missed the message of hope represented by the children in the programs. My perspective changed as I learned more, and Elaine was fortunate to be accepted in one of the programs that I had, at one point, so easily dismissed.

Gradually it became clear to me that my daughter's persistence (stubbornness) meant that as long as she wanted something, it was realistic to believe that she would reach her goal in time, and *that* was, and remains, a basis for hope.

PARENTING TWINS

I don't know how other twins behave, but my two were used to sharing space and craved it in the beginning. When we put the twins down for a nap or for the night, we put them on opposite ends of the crib. All on their own they would seek each other out and nestle close together. They never appeared to want to spend any time at their own end. When they graduated to separate cribs, we put the cribs next to each other, because when we initially had them separated in the nursery, both rocked back and forth in their cribs, attempting to "walk" the cribs closer together.

When they were still small enough to share one of those small plastic tubs used to bathe babies, we used it as an impromptu "pool" one hot summer day. A friend with a child their age came to visit. My two hopped out of the tub to say hi, and the other child stepped into the tub and sat down. Elaine joined him, and he let out a howl. He was not willing to share the space. My two were confused and then amused. They knew there was plenty of space!

As Louis and Elaine grew older and more mobile, they frequently would team up to overcome an obstacle. Once when my parents were "watching" them, they were surprised to find Elaine holding the legs of a chair as Louis stood on it attempting to get to the cookie jar on the counter. They were eighteen months old.

Elaine is a morning person and a social butterfly. Louis is at his best later in the day and is a bit more reticent. They have never competed with each other. Louis is fairly easy to get along with, but he knows how to "bug" his sister. In fact, one of the first expressions Elaine learned in American Sign Language was "bug off." Louis realized early in life that it would be a bad idea to try to fool Elaine by telling her something that would get her into trouble. As a result, she knows that when Louis says something, he means it.

It was Louis who figured out how to get Elaine to wear a warm coat instead of a light jacket when fall weather became colder. He had her stand on the deck in the light jacket for five minutes. She always came inside, told Louis he was right, and donned the appropriate outerwear. This belief that Louis was the truth teller and the one to be reckoned with continued as she matured. In the early days of Elaine's participation in the Special Olympics sailing program, her coach phoned me asking for an effective strategy to use to get Elaine to follow the rules. I suspect she thought just telling Elaine she was calling me would work. However, my response was that if Elaine knew she was going to phone Louis, Elaine would comply. That threat worked. Elaine understood that it was best to do what Louis said.

After four months of maternity leave, I returned to work, part time, as a teacher in a high school about twenty miles from our home. I had time to take Elaine to different therapy appointments, go to work, and then get back in mid-afternoon. Louis didn't go to the appointments with us, and as neither child went to work with me, I hired someone to watch the children during the day. Before Elaine was six months old, she was accepted in a program for infants and toddlers where she would get physical therapy, occupational therapy (fine motor skills), and speech therapy. She was provided transportation to and from the half day program. By the time Louis was old enough to go to a nursery school, he had no qualms about a half day program. He saw it as an opportunity to do new things and knew from watching his sister come and go that it was only a short time away from home.

• •

Looking back, I realize that having twins made a difference in how I dealt with Elaine. Both children accompanied me most places. At church I left both babies in the nursery so I could worship without distractions. Once, another mother asked me how I could just leave them in the nursery. My response was that it was good for them and for me to have a break for an hour.

TURNING A NEIGHBORHOOD INTO A COMMUNITY

When my husband was sent to the Middle East on an unaccompanied deployment, I knew I needed friends in our local neighborhood. During the late afternoon and early evenings when I walked the twins in the stroller, I looked for other mothers with young children. I found two and invited them to my home in the afternoon so that our children could play together. We met between 3:00 and 5:00 p.m. Mondays, Wednesdays, and Fridays. The playgroup started with three families and four children (three boys and one girl), but it grew as more babies came and when new families moved into the neighborhood. Mothers, and later nannies or au pairs, accompanied the children. It was not a drop-off program. No snacks were provided. It was just a time for children to play and mothers and caregivers to chat. Before departing, everything was picked up and put away. This playgroup turned a collection of houses into a community. It provided Elaine and Louis with playmates. When I began working full time, the playgroup continued. It ended five and a half years later when we moved to the Midwest.

One of the wonderful things about the playgroup was that Elaine was a full participant. Sometimes the children engaged in parallel play, but as they got comfortable with each other, they engaged with one another. Two memories of the playgroup illustrate this well. We decided to invite the playgroup to the twins' second birthday party.

Parents arrived with high chairs, which were arranged around the dining room table. Parents stood against the walls. Elaine, with her poor muscle tone, had to have pillows strategically placed so that she could remain upright. Her chair was next to Louis's chair on one side of the table. The cakes came out, "happy birthday" was sung, the candles were blown out, and the cakes sliced. When Elaine got her slice of cake, she bent over and pulled the plate with the cake on top of it toward her face and took a bite. Looking back at video taken that day, the amazing thing was that no one intervened or even seemed to notice. Elaine was just eating her cake all by herself. The fact that she didn't wait to have the cake served to her in spoonfuls shocked no one.

The other memory was three years later. It was getting close to the end of playgroup, and a father had arrived to pick up the nanny and his two sons for an appointment. He arrived just at the point that his eldest son was informing my daughter that she couldn't wear the stethoscope because girls can't be doctors. Elaine wasn't buying that logic, and neither did the father. He told his son he was lucky that he, and not his mother, was picking him up. Both parents were doctors at NIH. No one suggested that Elaine's disability should prevent her from doing this or that. That was the way it was in playgroup. Elaine was just one of the guys.

Long after the playgroup ended, I would sometimes run into parents of the children who came to my home. They always asked about Elaine and Louis and then talked about their own children and their children's many achievements. Sometimes the conversation involved a discussion about the challenges of raising teens and handling drugs and sex, problems I didn't have. Other times, the conversation was about school-related issues. One parent shared with me that when she faced educational challenges, she used techniques she learned from me. Those techniques apparently were, being polite, being very clear about desired outcomes, and being clear in the belief that thoughtful consideration by the faculty would lead to a successful solution. In other words, whatever the emotion, don't act on it; rather focus on the desired outcome.

The playgroup created a community within our neighborhood. That community had a positive impact on the parents and the children in ways that I never imagined when I issued the first invitations to come to play in my home.

THE MEDICAL WORLD AND A CHILD WITH A DEVELOPMENTAL DELAY

Looking back on the first months of Elaine's life, it felt as if we were going over a waterfall. All sorts of information came at us and we struggled to find our footing. Just when we felt we had landed, something new happened and we realized we had only been on a ledge and once again we were thrown down with the rushing water. It took a while to feel as though we had stabilized.

Initially, the doctors presented a challenge. As reported earlier, Elaine's first visit with a pediatrician started off poorly when he noted we had twins and stated that he would see the mongoloid first. He learned not to use that term and also began to learn along with us about protocols for children with Down syndrome. Information from the National Down Syndrome Congress was incredibly useful when doctors would say our concerns were misplaced as they were "normal" for infants with Down syndrome. The protocols helped doctors understand what was normal for an individual with Trisomy 21.

Elaine was born with cross-eyes and clogged tear ducts. I did not accept the statement that this was normal for someone with Trisomy 21, and once we were able to see an ophthalmologist, neither did he. When her blood work indicated she had an underactive thyroid, her pediatrician told us it was nothing to be concerned about. I wasn't convinced and asked if someone could explain it to me. A specialist was called and the physician and I learned that Elaine had an underactive thyroid and what that meant. She began taking medication that she still takes today.

And recall that we were told that we should try to do the best we could by her because when she reached the age of seven she would stop learning. That was motivation enough to learn and do as much as was feasible with Elaine. Then it became clear that the extra chromosome just meant it would take longer, but with patience Elaine could continue to develop new skills long after she was seven years old.

In those early years with Elaine, the doctors learned and so did we. Mostly I listened and then religiously followed up on every suggestion. At some point, I realized that the doctors were not going to go home with my child, and that some of their recommendations simply did not reflect that my child was a member of a loving family. At those times, I think doctors saw my child as dysfunctional eyes, ears, or whatever their specialty was, but they did not see her as an individual.

As a new mother, it didn't take much to question if I was doing enough for my children. Sometimes the comments of doctors contributed to the anxiety. When it comes to guilt, I believe new mothers have it in spades. I wish doctors were more sensitive to that! I remember sitting next to a woman in church who was distraught because the doctor told her that her child would suffer because there was no structure in the home. I asked her if she supervised her child's homework, if the family had dinner together, and if there were routines surrounding a bath and bedtime. She described her family's routines and began to understand that there was structure in her home. She felt better and began to sort out the message the doctor probably intended to convey.

Elaine had lots of issues that involved specialists and the occasional visit to the emergency room. Before the age of two, Elaine had a procedure to open her clogged tear ducts, experienced a profound hearing loss that required hearing aids for both ears and had several procedures to insert PE (pressure equalization) tubes, and was hospitalized for pneumonia. The specialists saw the need, but the challenge was accessing them, as each specialist had skillful gatekeepers adept at protecting their bosses.

• •

The doctor who operated to open her clogged tear ducts was very sympathetic, but it took persistence to get an initial appointment to see him. Because Elaine's primary physician was reluctant to refer her, I called the doctor's office. His secretary rebuffed my efforts by phone, so I walked into the office one morning with Elaine. I was fortunate that the doctor came into the reception area because he heard the secretary raise her voice. He took one look at Elaine and ushered us into his office. He did not think clogged tear ducts were normal for Down syndrome patients, and he also expressed concern about her crossed eyes. Elaine had surgery on her tear ducts and ended up with glasses to straighten her eyes.

The audiologist recommended PE tubes to help with Elaine's profound hearing loss. The Eustachian tubes in her ears were so tiny that she had a conductive hearing loss that typically ends as the child grows older. However, in the interest of developing normal speech, PE tubes can be inserted and provide the conductivity needed. The young doctors actually performing the procedure thought it was a waste of their time to insert the tubes because there was no infection in Elaine's ears. They never understood the link between the small size of her Eustachian tubes and her conductive hearing loss.

It was easy getting the doctor to schedule the procedure, but a bit daunting to pass the screening the day of the procedure. The one time I could not take her to the procedure (tubes were inserted, popped out as she grew, and new ones had to be inserted), I warned her father to affirm that she did not have a cold, had not eaten or had anything to drink, etc. I told him that if he hesitated or waffled they would send the two of them home. When he returned after the new PE tubes had been inserted, he told me that most everyone else had been turned away because the parents hadn't responded to the screening questions with confidence. He also told me that the doctor told him that there had been no fluid in the ear and was not certain why the tubes had been considered necessary. The lesson is to understand the reason for the surgery and to be steadfast so it takes place!

In the instance of the pneumonia, Elaine did not appear to have the classic symptoms (no fever, no fluid in the lungs), so the doctors were just plain irritated that I insisted her ragged breathing demanded attention. Because her father had experienced medical issues involving testing for oxygen in the blood, I persuaded an intern to have her blood tested for oxygen levels. Just as the head of the ER asked the MPs to escort us out of the ER (no kidding!) the intern returned with the test results. The test showed Elaine was in acute respiratory distress and an entire team sprang into action. She was hospitalized with pneumonia, put in an oxygen tent, and because they could not figure out which type of pneumonia she had, they treated her as if she had viral and bacterial pneumonia. She was in the hospital for just under a week.

Elaine developed allergic reactions to penicillin while still in elementary school. She was at school and complained of pain. The nurse called home and the au pair called me. By the time I arrived to pick Elaine up, her feet and legs were extremely swollen. A trip to the clinic led to the diagnosis of an allergic reaction to the penicillin she was taking for an ear infection. This inability to take penicillin was just one more thing to add to her medical chart.

One week later, Louis was at the orthodontist when he complained about pain in his feet. Before he even removed his shoes, it was clear his ankles were swollen. We went from that appointment directly to the doctor's. It took a while to confirm, but we learned that evening that Louis also had an allergic reaction to penicillin.

When she was eleven, Elaine woke up early one morning crying in pain. She would not sit up in bed, let alone walk or stand, so I carried her to the emergency room at our clinic. She was seen immediately. The diagnosis was a dislocated hip. She was sent to a hospital to have it treated because the doctors feared she might go into respiratory distress if she had the procedure to put it back into the socket while anesthetized. She did experience respiratory problems, but at the hospital they were prepared, and her hip was pulled back into the socket without Elaine experiencing any more pain. She was not hospitalized, which apparently is unusual. But she was cheerful and

• •

no longer experiencing pain, so there was no need. However, we were sent home with instructions to follow up with an orthopedic surgeon. Getting a consult to see this specialist didn't take too long, but it took a while for me to understand what the doctors had discovered as a result of the dislocated hip.

I learned that Elaine was born with only one hip socket on her left side. Her right leg was held to the pelvic girdle with ligaments. There was no shelf for the hip joint, and the joint itself was fused to the leg bone, not tilted as it should be. The hip she did have had spontaneously popped out of the socket in her sleep. Once the issue of the dislocated hip was resolved, and because she had no pain on her right side, the surgeon decided the best course of action was to monitor the situation.

In the next few months, Elaine began to grow and the ligaments holding her right leg to the pelvis were stretched, causing acute pain. Many individuals with Down syndrome have a high tolerance for pain, and that is certainly true of my daughter. Apparently the low muscle tone causes a delayed reaction to pain. In any event, by the time Elaine feels pain, the condition causing the pain is generally very severe. Over the next six months, the episodes of extreme pain came more frequently. The decision was finally made to schedule surgery to create a hip socket. The surgery would also involve creating a shelf in the pelvic bone and cutting the leg bone just below the ball so that it would fit into the new socket. This was a surgery that would take several hours and would involve several days in the hospital. She would be put in a body cast from her nipples to her knees and would remain in the cast until the bones healed. I was told to plan to stay by my daughter's side as she recovered from the surgery. When she came home she would need to remain in a hospital bed for about three months and then use a walker.

I got leave from work for the week of the surgery. I also arranged to have one of our favorite au pairs return from Germany to help out as Louis could not be left at home alone when I stayed up to a week with Elaine in the hospital. Everything was ready when forty-eight hours before the surgery her primary physician called me at home to share his deep reservations about the surgery. He said he had made calls to two doctors familiar with orthopedic surgery who were experienced in caring for individuals with Down syndrome. Neither doctor had returned his calls, but he knew the surgery would be very painful and he worried that in the end, it might not work. He cited the incidence of bone re-absorption following a more common surgery to correct problems in the neck region. He advised me to cancel the surgery but promised to call once he spoke with the two experts in the field.

His call sent me into a panic because both the surgeon and pediatrician were wonderful doctors. And, of course, everything was set for the surgery. I had taken leave, prepped the substitute for my classes, and the au pair had arrived from Germany for the duration of Elaine's hospitalization. What a dilemma! Should I follow the advice of a wonderful physician and change all the plans or go ahead with the surgery? I knew that the window for the surgery was narrow because Elaine had begun to grow. It was surgery as scheduled or no surgery at all.

I called the children's father and explained the options. He deferred the decision to me. I called others in my family, and my brother's son-in-law, an orthopedic surgeon, listened to me and gently guided me to a decision. By the time I went to bed, I chose to go ahead with the surgery because Elaine was refusing to walk, and as a result she would most likely end up in a wheelchair, with a more limited—and possibly shorter—life. Even if the surgery didn't take, I would know that I had tried my best for her. Surgery was the answer.

I received a phone call in the very early hours the next morning from Elaine's primary physician. He called to say that he had spoken to both doctors and they both told him the surgery was a good idea. I was glad he had called because now all the doctors treating her were in agreement. During our phone call I told him that I had decided to go ahead with the surgery before I went to bed the previous night. He was not at all surprised and said, "I taught you well."

. . . .

This wonderful doctor had indeed coached me and helped me understand that as a parent I was an important member of the team supporting Elaine.

Prior to the surgery, Elaine was in a room with several adults who were also waiting to be taken in for their surgeries. She was the only child. She had earphones on with her cassette recorder nearby and sang "Somewhere over the Rainbow" along with her tape. The mood in the room was somber and tense, but then folks began to chuckle as they heard her singing. Elaine continued to sing as she was wheeled into surgery. Her mood lightened the atmosphere in the room and eased my own anxiety.

Once the surgery was over and Elaine was awake, I was allowed to visit her in the post- op room. The nurse attending her said Elaine told her, "No french fries for you!" which the nurse guessed was Elaine's way of swearing. She was correct; Elaine was not at all happy, but she eventually nodded off. I saw her next when she went into her own room, and I stayed with her.

The morning after the surgery, she went white, groaned quietly, and was clearly in pain. I stepped into the hall and asked a nurse to call the doctor. The nurse told me everyone was too busy and we would just have to cope. Happily, the technician who made and cut off casts happened to be in the hall, heard the conversation, and asked the nurse to join him by my daughter's bedside. He explained to the nurse that Elaine had a high tolerance for pain and that if she was in pain, someone needed to help her. The technician took his saw and cut along the side of the cast, lifting the top part of the cast and releasing the pressure. The nurse was startled by the blood blisters that had formed because of the swelling. Elaine was so pleased to have the pressure released that she began joking with the cast technician. The lesson here is that someone with a high tolerance for pain and limited language needs an advocate close at hand.

Before the surgery, I had talked with Elaine about what would happen during the surgery and about what would happen after the surgery. I also took her to see a cast being put on and taken off, but

. . . .

she didn't understand until the moment the pressure was released that the cast wasn't permanent.

Getting her home from the hospital required careful thought. In a cast from her nipples to her knees, with a bar between her upper thighs to make it possible for her to pee and poop, Elaine was not easy to carry. The doctors wanted us to use a wheelchair, but even with the back of the seat flattened, the cast made it impossible for Elaine to be supported. The au pair suggested using our plastic sled, and that worked, providing support for her head and neck and giving those carrying her something to hold other than the cast when lifting and carrying her. I had a minivan and we took out the backseats so she could rest comfortably during the ride home. We had already set up a hospital bed in the living room, figuring it was located in the center of things, and Elaine would not feel isolated. Neighbors helped get her from the car into the house, and they repeated the favor every time we had to return to the hospital for a checkup or re-casting.

Prior to the surgery, Elaine was seventy-five pounds and 3'8", so even with the body cast, it was possible to lift her. After the surgery, her legs were almost an inch different in length. A second surgery on the knee of her longer leg prevented the bones in that leg from growing, and eventually the knees on both legs aligned. However, before the knees aligned, in addition to needing shoe orthotics, the sole of her right shoe had to be built up. This was not inexpensive.

The shoe store we frequented helped us find shoes that could be altered in this way and even found dressy shoes so she could be free of the walking shoes on special occasions. It was a blessing to work with sales staff in retail stores who had empathy. It was a happy day when the short leg caught up with the longer leg.

Following the surgery, Elaine's iron levels were closely monitored. Because of the cuts made to the bones during the surgery, the doctors were worried about anemia. She was given lots of iron supplements with no noticeable results. Finally, an endoscopy was scheduled because malabsorption (specifically caused by Celiac Sprue) was suspected. Celiac Sprue is a gluten-sensitive enteropathy, a chronic disorder of the digestive tract that results in an inability to tolerate gliadin, the alcohol-soluble fraction of gluten. Gluten is a protein commonly found in wheat, rye, and barley. The procedure was supposed to take no more than twenty minutes, but no one came to see me for two hours! When the doctor finally came, they told me there was good news and bad news. I asked for the good news first. I was told she didn't have cancer. I said that I never expected cancer at all, so what was the bad news? At that point, I learned why two hours had elapsed. Apparently there were no cilia at all in her intestinal track. The absence of cilia is indication of Celiac Sprue. It was so unusual to see no cilia that interns in the clinic had been paged to view the procedure.

We left the clinic knowing that Elaine had full-blown Celiac Sprue. In the first six months after ridding her diet of gluten, Elaine grew twelve inches and gained thirty pounds. She is now 4'8" and will not grow taller, but nothing stops her from gaining weight.

Another medical event occurred when Elaine was in her twenties. She woke up in tears complaining of acute pain in her abdomen. It looked like the pain was excruciating. Again, we went to the ER at the local hospital. She was seen immediately as it was visibly clear she was in acute pain. She was hospitalized and a series of tests were performed ruling out all sorts of things. On the third morning in the hospital she asked if she could go home. On that morning, she was no longer in pain and she was released. The team treating her gave me the printouts of all the tests so that if the pain reoccurred, those same tests would not be repeated. No one knew what had caused the pain, and it remains a mystery.

It isn't easy to find a doctor who specializes in Down syndrome, but Elaine has been followed for several years by someone who is an expert in the field. This opportunity came about because of something I wish had never happened. Elaine took ice cream from a self-serve machine at a cafeteria where she volunteered. The agency supporting her during the day said she could not return to the agency until a behavior modification plan was developed by a doctor. Our HMO sent us to their mental-health clinic and the sociologist who saw us ordered an IQ test. I knew that an IQ test would not lead to a behavior modification plan, so I asked if there was a psychiatrist who would speak briefly with me. There was, he did, and he referred us to the Down Syndrome Clinic at Kennedy Krieger in Baltimore, Maryland.

When we first went to the clinic in Baltimore, I learned some surprising things about my daughter. First, I learned she was compulsive and depressed. Apparently the language skills we worked on did not help her express her emotions. As I already knew, she needed help identifying and understanding boundaries. The doctor also suspected she had sleep apnea because she was chatting away with him when suddenly she nodded off. We left that initial meeting with a prescription to help with her depression and compulsive behaviors, a schedule of sessions working with the Circles Curriculum to work on boundary issues, and a referral for a sleep study. The sleep study showed that she does, indeed, have sleep apnea, and for several years she has used a CPAP every night. The machine travels with her on trips, and she is very good about using it.

So medically, Elaine has an underactive thyroid (takes a pill), sleep apnea (uses a CPAP), Celiac Sprue (maintains a gluten-free diet), an allergy to penicillin (avoids it at all costs), and compulsive behaviors and depression that are treated with medication. After the hip surgery she had inserts placed in her shoes and lifts added on the sole of her right shoe. She still wears inserts to align her feet properly but no longer needs lifts on the right shoe. Once she started to grow, her hearing improved and she no longer needed hearing aids or PE tubes. She wears glasses and has done for most of her life. Because of her weight gain, she is monitored closely for signs of diabetes, but so far that is not an issue with which we must contend.

THE GOOD PATIENT

Elaine isn't afraid of needles, which is a good thing because with an underactive thyroid she frequently has blood drawn. When she was younger she would sit still in the lab chair, hold out her arm, and request a colorful Band-Aid as her reward. In all her trips to the clinic and the emergency room, she followed the procedure of weigh-ins, temperature, and blood pressure—in that order. When we went to a new clinic, Elaine preferred the same sequence. I would ask the nurses that if they were going to weigh her, take her temperature, and check her blood pressure, to do them in that order. Having a routine helps ease the anxiety of a visit to the ER or clinic.

Elaine's very first surgery required pre-op tests in a military clinic. She was really just a baby and would not keep still, so the doctors put her on a papoose board—essentially binding her to a board. After that experience Elaine kept her body rigid and absolutely still to avoid ever repeating the experience of being restricted in that manner. This always amazed doctors, but Elaine understood the consequence of moving during an exam, and complied with the request to be still.

DENTISTS

Elaine was very wary of anyone working in her mouth. Her first dentist was exceptionally patient and never rushed her. He said he practiced gentle dentistry and he certainly helped Elaine overcome any fears. Initially, she made her brother go first while she sat outside the door and peeked in. Getting her into the dentist's chair meant I had to stand where she could see me. Finally, she developed a rapport with the doctor and looked forward to the six-month checkups.

One time when I was having my own dental checkup, the dentist shared a story about Elaine with me. His practice had expanded and new staff had been hired. One morning, the new receptionist complained that "someone has been playing with the phone." He asked the receptionist what she meant. He listened to the recorded message and told the receptionist that no one was playing with the phone. It was a patient (Elaine) trying to make an appointment. He asked her to call back and schedule a time for Elaine to come in. She had not done so by the time of my appointment, so it was made before I left his office. I worried when he retired how Elaine would cope, but she has had no qualms about seeing the new dentist, based on her good experience with the first. The key seems to be that the dentist treated her as an individual and did not focus on her disability.

THE MEDICAL WORLD AND LOUIS

Louis had a different relationship with doctors. He feared needles so much that he would not tell me when he felt ill until he was truly sick. By the time he shared his concerns with me and we got to the doctor's, his anxiety over needles was the least of our problems. When he was seven, he fell ill with something that took hold, and it seemed to me that it might be a long time before he felt well again. He was miserable.

For some reason, I imagined getting him a pet would help. That is how Petey entered our lives. Petey was a beagle who had been well trained (thank heavens), but his owners had been told that to ensure the wife's safe pregnancy, Petey had to go. Petey went from a home where he slept in an open cage in the basement to ours where he shared the bed with Louis! By the end of the week with Petey, Louis was on the mend, his lethargy was gone, and he returned to school.

By the time Louis was ten, he was on various medications to treat Tourette's syndrome, medications he had to take on a schedule. Some had to be taken midday at the nurse's office at school. This necessity to go to the nurse is hard on young people as it identifies them as different. Middle school and high school are tough places to be different. Happily, understanding doctors helped us find a solution so that the medicines he took in the morning lasted through the school day.

Louis's medications were a challenge for his dad. One time his dad tossed all of Louis's pills out the first day of a visit. Without the medication, Louis was unable to control his tics, and I got a call from his Dad demanding that I send more medication as soon as possible. Louis was on medications that were strictly controlled, so in the end his father had to speak directly with the doctor to get a new prescription. That was the last time medications were tossed out. His dad wasn't so different from many who claim that our young are overmedicated. It may be true for some, but in my son's situation, being off the medication makes its need obvious.

Louis attended a weeklong youth leadership conference the summer between his junior and senior year in high school. One morning Louis, along with everyone in the group, sat impatiently on a bus waiting for two stragglers. As the stragglers approached the bus, apparently Louis realized he had forgotten to take his "meds." Louis's roommate said the entire group spontaneously said, "Louis, we'll wait!" His roommate shared this with me when relating stories about how "cool" my son was. In my son's case, the medications *had* a positive impact. I used the past tense, because once out of school, Louis has had more control over his activities and has chosen not to take medication. He still deals with Tourette's syndrome, but the type of job and the kind of activities he enjoys mean that there is less anxiety, and the symptoms of the disorder are manageable.

SCHOOLS

Elaine went to an Easter Seals Program about two miles from our home when she was still an infant. When she aged out of the program, we enrolled her in the Montessori preschool her brother attended. The Montessori program provided many opportunities, but there was no speech therapy provided in the program, so we had to pay for this privately. I was encouraged to petition the District of Columbia schools for therapy services. The DC schools offered Elaine therapy on the condition that she would attend a program in a public school in another part of the city. That program was housed in a high school and had four young adult males said to be functioning at the chronological age of four. This proposed placement led to a hearing at the district's administrative offices. I had a lawyer present and a statement from the teacher of the program where Elaine was to be placed. The teacher questioned the safety of a five-year-old female being placed in a program with eighteen-year-old males.

The hearing officer was incredulous. He ruled that Elaine was entitled to services and could stay at her preschool. We won, but the speech therapist providing the services did not get paid, and when we asked why, were told we needed to appeal. Apparently, we won at the city level and had to proceed to the state level. We did not realize that Washington, D.C. had a city and state level of government! Since we were moving out of the area, we paid the therapist but did not appeal.

Other than the private preschool and Louis's one year in an independent school in the Midwest, both children have been in public schools. There were many opportunities to advocate for both children once they entered school, but because I was a teacher, somehow it was easier to anticipate challenges and build productive relationships. However, I too had to press administrators when their take on the law differed from my understanding. Typically, I would ask to which law they were referring. At the time I knew the federal laws, the state laws, and district regulations and policies, so just asking politely often helped move the discussion from "I know" to "let's check."

One time I went directly to the central office of the school district because I was told my son could not access technology until he could use a keyboard correctly. Because his disability involved difficulty manipulating pen and pencil, as you might imagine, the keyboard was daunting for him. It was a relief to find that the district owned technology appropriate for him and he was eligible to use it with the skills he had.

When advocating for my children in the school, I tried to treat my colleagues the way I wished to be treated when a parent of one of my students was upset with me. It wasn't always easy to remain calm, but focusing on a positive outcome for my children helped me keep my composure. When Louis was in the third grade, the IEP meeting (annual meeting to develop the Individualized Education Plan) was particularly challenging. The meeting began on an unbelievably negative note. Although Louis's third grade report card showed great grades and his standardized testing affirmed his areas of weakness as well as his strengths, his classroom teacher's first comment was "your son is so stupid, he cannot even pronounce his own name."

Think about that statement. I know our last name, Fickenscher, is difficult to pronounce, but I have never met a child who was unable to correctly say his or her own name. Louis was at the meeting and was visibly shaken. The room was silent and I found the strength to introduce myself, and explained that while others might put the accent on the first syllable, our family did not. The teacher did not apologize, but the tone of the meeting shifted.

Another particularly difficult time was my son's first year in middle school. The middle school had a new program specifically designed for students deemed gifted with learning disabilities. Louis was among the first students in the program. Initially, he was placed in classes for the gifted, where the teachers thought he was either lazy or disabled. Then they moved him into classes for the learning disabled where the teachers thought he didn't fit. It wasn't clear that the program was specifically for those with areas of giftedness as well as learning disabilities. His IEP from elementary school clearly outlined the accommodations he needed, but the general consensus of the middle school teachers seemed to be that Louis was lazy.

When treating my colleagues as I wished to be treated didn't work, I asked a colleague what I could do to cast Louis in a different light. She urged me to consult a specific psychiatrist familiar with the school district. The cost was significant, but my friend told me that the school district respected the psychiatrist and would pay attention to his report. When I first spoke to the psychiatrist, I was very clear about what I hoped would be presented in the final report. He told me that he would base the report on the outcome of the tests, not my wishes. The testing was done, and when it was delivered, the psychiatrist confirmed that I really understood my son. The recommendations in the report were exactly what I had hoped for.

I delivered copies of the document to the members of the team scheduled to meet before the beginning of the second year at the school. We met, but had to reschedule because most at the meeting had not even looked at the report. When we finally met again, the head of the school's special education department asked what I wanted his teachers to do. I said that the accommodations identified in his IEP, which had been reaffirmed by the report from the psychiatrist, were within the tool kit of most classroom teachers. It was time to begin providing those accommodations. Although that fall things did change in a positive way for Louis, middle school still remained a struggle.

• •

Right to a Full Life

When Louis went to high school, life improved significantly. The head of the special education department was creative and managed to place Louis in courses where both the teacher and the students enjoyed having him in class. There were challenges, of course, but both teachers and administrators were willing to work with him to resolve issues as they came up.

When Louis was a sophomore he was suspended from school. If they could have sent him home, they would have, but as they were unable to reach me, he sat in the detention center and came home on his regular bus. When I got home, Louis told me he had been suspended for three days. He had been in an altercation, and in our district anyone involved in a fight is suspended. I asked him to write an email to his principal apologizing for his actions, but not to send it before I read it. While I read it, I told Louis he needed to start working on his homework as he would probably be returning to school in the morning. Shortly after the email was sent, the principal called and asked both of us to report to her office in the morning before Louis went back to class.

Louis had written about being in the cafeteria and how he was asked by another boy to throw food at someone sitting across the table from him. Louis said no; the other boy stated that individual sitting across from Louis was a retard. Louis replied that this wasn't true; the young man had no disabilities. When asked how he knew that, Louis said his sister had Down syndrome. At that point, the young man knocked Louis's hand, and then threw food at Louis .

The personnel maintaining order in the cafeteria had to sort out what happened, so Louis and the other boy were escorted to the assistant principal's office. When Louis was asked if he had done something to initiate the fight, Louis said he supposed so, because he believed people were always getting irritated with him.

At the intake interview, we learned that some of his teachers had come to Louis's defense stating there was no way Louis would initiate a fight, and that most likely he wouldn't even defend himself in a fight. We also learned that on his bus going home he was applauded by the driver in the mistaken belief that Louis had been suspended for defending himself. The assistant principal began to realize that had she asked more follow-up questions, she would have uncovered more of the "story." Louis went back to class. Two days later he met with the other young man who was just returning to school after his suspension. They shook hands and promised to avoid each other in the future—and they did.

WELCOMED AND INCLUDED

Elaine attended a regular Montessori preschool and then public schools. She didn't attend special classes. It was a challenge getting her into the Montessori school, but once we got Elaine in, everyone was wonderful in making accommodations when she needed them. I think the idea of having a child with a cognitive delay was more challenging than the reality of actually having Elaine in class. It made it so much easier when it was clear we measured progress in small steps. It helped that I raised money for the school, and I was happy to brainstorm solutions to problems as they cropped up with Elaine.

One concern was that Elaine often needed to visit the bathroom, but how could she be trusted to go across the hall and back on her own? I called the head of a wonderful preschool on the other side of the city that welcomed individuals with developmental delays. The suggestion I passed along was to cut out paper footsteps and tape them on the floor to and from the restroom. This solution also helped other children who sometimes got lost, and it helped make clear that Elaine was more alike than different. Just as things were progressing smoothly at the Montessori preschool, my husband's job took us to the Midwest.

We only lived in St Louis, Missouri, for a year, but the school Elaine attended in kindergarten was transforming. There was no struggle to get her in and no need to raise funds or for me to take on any major responsibility at the school in order to keep her there. She was welcomed. Being welcomed is so much better than being accepted or tolerated. It frees you to be part of a team, to listen to constructive criticism, and to problem solve. There were challenges, but no one called me at home expecting me to fix it. Sometimes I heard about the situation after a successful resolution had been found. Sometimes I was part of the brainstorming that led to a solution.

By the end of the first month, I wrote a letter to the principal thanking everyone for welcoming my daughter. He read the letter in a faculty meeting and told me about it the next morning. Apparently some of the teachers of the upper grades were worried that once students with disabilities passed out of the "cute" stage, they would be difficult to teach and even dangerous to have in the classroom. He said that beginning the meeting by reading my letter shifted the tone of what had promised to be a difficult meeting, which is why the principal thanked me the next day. It was a learning experience for all of us that year, and my daughter flourished.

I particularly enjoyed one IEP meeting. As we began the meeting, the tension around the table was palpable. It quickly became apparent that the tension had nothing to do with me or with Elaine. The teachers were frustrated with a policy regarding the use of the intercom. The teachers wanted to be able to ask staff to step in the hall when one of the kindergarteners (not necessarily Elaine) strayed out of class. The administrator agreed and the tension dissipated. No one looked to me for a solution.

That year, I walked Elaine to school, just a few blocks away. Over the course of the first few weeks, other children joined us. I felt a bit like the Pied Piper leading the children. When we arrived at school, we all sat together on the steps waiting for the doors to open. The children talked, told jokes, and were happy to enter the building once the doors opened.

The school fully included Elaine and so did her classmates' parents. The girls in her class joined the Daisy Scout Troop I led, and Elaine was included in birthday parties and other events. Our neighbors also welcomed her. Although we were new to the neighborhood, it was a very welcoming one. In no time at all, the son of our next door neighbors started coming to the house to wait for the procession to school to start. When my marriage dissolved and it was clear my children and I would be returning to the DC area, several of the children who walked with us each morning asked me how they would get to school in the fall. We talked it over and they agreed they were ready to walk by themselves.

In St Louis we sent Louis to a private school instead of the public school attended by Elaine. We had concerns about his performance in the last months at the Montessori school and hoped that a fresh start without Elaine in the mix might help. Louis loved the new school, but the principal called before the end of the first month to ask me to come in and talk with his teachers as they had concerns. When I went to observe Louis in his class before the meeting, he was totally unaware of what was going on around him. He was "zoned out" in his own world. Later that month we got a diagnosis of Attention Deficit Disorder and he began to take medication that helped him focus. His teachers were creative and willing to work with Louis and with us. Louis enjoyed his school.

Meanwhile, I explored various support groups in our corner of St Louis. At one meeting, parents of children with significant developmental delays were talking about moving to another city because they were so frustrated battling the school district. When I talked about my daughter's experience at a local school they were very interested until they learned the name of the school. My daughter attended a school that was truly diverse. Just like our Montessori experience, the school was a definite racial and ethnic mix. Caucasians did not constitute the majority. I pointed out to the parents that if we wanted our children with developmental and intellectual disabilities to be included, we needed to embrace inclusion of others. This remains true.

After a year in St Louis, divorce meant the twins and I returned to Maryland because I could return to a job that would, along with child support, help me make ends meet. Both Louis and Elaine would attend school in the district where I taught. To be honest, I picked the house where I rented because it was near an elementary school that had a program of inclusion. At that time, most schools mainstreamed special education students, which meant they ate lunch and had art and music with the regular education students, but spent the bulk of the day in special classes. At this particular elementary school, all students attended class together.

When I went to register the children, I was told that I would have to go through the screening process and the district would place both children in appropriate programs. I pointed out that they both had IEPs that were current and we lived across the street from the school. I was referred to the Area Administrator to resolve the issue.

I went to the area office where I was told the person I needed to see was out. I said it was OK, that we would wait. When the administrator returned, it was a woman I knew, who listened to what I wanted. She was surprised that I had not been able to enroll the children. She told me she would make the necessary calls, but to wait an hour before returning to the school. We did, the IEPs were accepted, and Louis and Elaine were enrolled with no further issues.

In grades 1 through 5, Elaine and Louis attended this elementary school. A special education teacher assisted in Elaine's classroom, but Elaine was not pulled out. I learned later that at one point they tried to have her leave the room for math and reading help, but she refused to go. As a result, they created new groups for reading and math. Others who weren't entitled to special education services, but who needed help in math and reading, were put in her reading and math group.

After the first year, I received phone calls from parents in late summer asking which teacher Elaine was scheduled to have. Imagine my surprise when I discovered that parents wanted their children to be in the same class with my daughter because they could join Elaine's groups and receive extra support. It was wonderful to discover that having my daughter as a classmate was considered an asset and not a liability.

Being fully included helped with problem resolution. In elementary school my daughter practically had a chair named for her in the principal's office. Because I was the leader of the Daisy and then

Brownie Troop at the school, I knew that her classmates had some ideas about how to solve that problem. Elaine and I asked them to attend the annual IEP meeting when progress on goals is reviewed and new ones are identified for the coming year. First we had to overcome the principal's objections. The principal was convinced that inviting Elaine's classmates violated some policy, and it took a call from the central office of the school district before we could extend an invitation to her classmates.

IEP meetings can be formidable. The special education teacher explained its purpose and escorted the third graders into the room at the beginning of the meeting, He introduced them and explained that the meeting was about setting goals for Elaine and asked what they wanted for their friend. These third graders stated that they wanted Elaine to be able to stay in class and not be sent out. They wondered why, with three third grade classes, Elaine and the student always getting into trouble with her were always placed in the same class. After thanking them for their input, the third graders returned to their class, and the meeting continued. As a result of their wise suggestion, Elaine and her "trouble" buddy were separated. Elaine's behavior improved and she was no longer a regular visitor to the main office. The classmates made a positive contribution to Elaine's IEP and to their class.

In middle school and high school, inclusion did not work. When she was included in regular classes, she was ignored, but once she moved into the special education program there was little interaction with the regular program. Because she had been fully included in elementary school, her friends from elementary school kept us informed about school events, including class pictures. The bus stop was (and still is) right in front of our house. Elaine was supposed to ride the special education bus, but in middle school she insisted on riding the "regular" bus instead. One morning her friends at the bus stop marched Elaine right back to the front door and asked why she wasn't wearing something special. Apparently pictures were being taken that day and they were looking out for their friend! That is the legacy of full inclusion!

Her program in high school was located in the building where I was a teacher. The summer prior to Elaine's arrival, I hired a student in one of my classes to "teach Elaine how to be fifteen." The student asked what I meant. I told her that helping Elaine understand that it wasn't cool to stick her finger up her nose, scratch private parts, etc. would really help. What Elaine learned from that peer was invaluable. She arrived in high school knowing a number of students in the regular program. She felt like she belonged.

When Elaine heard an announcement about auditions for the school musical, she rounded up some friends and they all showed up at the auditions. The drama director included Elaine and her classmates in the cast, no speaking parts, but on stage and some crowd scenes. There were concerns about supervision during afternoon rehearsals, but I was able to promise that someone would always be on hand to provide that oversight. During the time backstage, Elaine and her friends hung out with the other actors and stagehands. Participating in the musical was a positive experience for everyone, and one that was repeated each year she attended that school.

In Elaine's first year in high school, some of the students in my government class wondered why the students in the special education program were so isolated. My regular education students created a club with the goal of providing opportunities for Elaine and her classmates to participate in school activities without the supervision of parents or special education teachers. They began with a lunch bunch where everyone gathered at lunch in a room off the cafeteria and ate, talked, and worked on a simple craft. The craft was to help break the ice, and the separate space for the group made it possible to move about and talk without the crowded conditions in the cafeteria. The idea expanded to school wide activities. It definitely helped that I could discuss my own concerns about leaving my daughter with one of them during a football game. Would they stay with her, accompany her to the bathroom—should she need to go—and not desert her if their friends came along? Once the students understood the level of commitment they were making for the duration of the game, many had no hesitation at all about being the buddy for the evening. Friendships developed and the students who participated learned that even with disabilities, Elaine and her classmates were more alike than different.

When I moved to a different job and was no longer at the school, the interaction between the special education and regular students did not continue. Part of the problem was that the faculty leader did not have a child with a special need and wasn't comfortable discussing what to expect when working with peers with disabilities.

For example, as a parent, I knew that my daughter wanted a boyfriend. From teen years onwards girls hope to find a boyfriend and the boys a girlfriend. Often male peers without disabilities do not know how to respond when my daughter asks "Do you have a girlfriend. The best response to my daughter's question is *yes*. Yes, indicates that the individual is going to be a friend, not a potential date. This heads off all sorts of problems. Because the faculty member wasn't comfortable discussing things like this, the regular education students drifted away and the program just petered out.

However, the parents of Elaine's classmates figured out ways to encourage social interaction and activities outside of school. There were parties before dances at various homes, activities on the weekends, and other gatherings. Elaine aged out of school in 2005, but she and the core group of friends from the special education class still get together regularly. The mother of one of Elaine's classmates sponsors an activity that meets in the activity room of her church one evening a month during the school year. It involves dinner and a craft and sometimes a dance. That group is one of Elaine's significant communities. And the student who taught Elaine about how to be fifteen became a teacher and moved into a condo two blocks from Elaine's place. She is again part of Elaine's life.

· ·

LIFE AFTER HIGH SCHOOL

Negotiating the world of special needs after Elaine exited school has been a challenge. One big problem was that until the age of twenty-one, Elaine was entitled to a free education in the public schools. After the age of twenty-one, services are based on eligibility and availability.

Elaine was eligible, though it was necessary to prove the level of her disability. In our state there is a Transitioning Youth Initiative, which meant that she wasn't dropped after she exited school. She was eligible for services and thus able to maintain her skills and learn new ones. Understanding what is actually available in terms of services and supports is often challenging. There isn't much stability in the world of Developmental Disability Administrations, and often the people who should know about programs are fairly new to their positions. While national advocacy groups can outline the "big picture," the regulations related to eligibility vary by state as do the services. In addition, most states have a huge waiting list for those services.

Knowledge of the Developmental Disability Administration in one's state is vital. It is also important to understand the dollar amount attached to the services a young adult receives. Although I was told that information about Elaine's funds was included the papers we received upon exiting public school, that fact was not true in my situation. It took persistence to learn the actual amount. This information continues to be critical. The funds follow my daughter, should she choose to move from one agency to another or to leave agencies altogether and self-direct her own services.

Several years ago it became increasingly frustrating trying to work with one of the agencies supporting my daughter. As a result, I decided to investigate what was then called New Directions (now it is labeled the Self-Directed Waiver). Under New Directions the individual with the disability becomes the employer. A non-disabled individual (support broker) provides support in the form of assistance with hiring, firing, and supervising employees and works with a financial management service to ensure that employees are paid. I received the required training to be a support broker. A team of people who knew Elaine met to develop a plan with her that would use her funds to provide the supports she needed to live the life she wanted. The funds were shifted from the agencies to Elaine's Self-Directed account. She doesn't have a large budget, but there is minimal overhead. When we were supported by the agencies, she had approximately fifteen hours of service a week. That first year under self-direction she averaged thirty hours a week, and more importantly, she was able to pay a wage that was competitive. As a result, the job coach and counselor (now called personal support) she hired in 2009 are still with her today. That continuity has made a huge difference in the quality of her life. As her support broker, I advocated for services, but it is far easier because we had a clear understanding of her budget. Elaine enjoys having control over her life. I enjoy the easy communication with and among the team supporting my daughter. Initially her brother took over the role of support broker, so that he cold learn what was involved. Then we hired a friend who is experienced with budgets and knows Elaine to be the Support Broker. Having a support broker who knows the self-advocate and can monitor the budget is ideal.

Improved communication with and among the individuals supporting Elaine is one important aspect of being in self-direction. Another important factor is that when we went to self-direction and left agencies, there was more one-on-one support. This means that when Elaine is in the community, she is not one of several—she is "it." Her personal supports and job coach support her, but they also help her develop relationships in the activities she engages in. Elaine is not just physically in the community; she is socially integrated as well. When she moved out of the family home, she basically changed her residence. She already had activities and jobs in the community, and if anything, is now closer to them.

PERSPECTIVE

Having children with special needs taught me the importance of humor. Just when it feels overwhelming, it helps to find something to laugh about. I remember a late afternoon appointment at a medical clinic. The doctor had just finished with Elaine's checkup when he was called out of the room for a consult. An intern remained with us and began taking information about my son. As the attention shifted away from Elaine, she became restless, and in an effort to get her to sit still, I told her that we would get french fries when the appointment was over if she would just behave a little longer.

The intern looked shocked and said, "I can't believe you would bribe a child!"

The doctor returned at that moment and his comment was, "That isn't bribery; that is positive reinforcement." Everyone laughed. It wasn't long before we left the clinic and got those french fries.

When someone receives government funds due to a disability, it is necessary periodically to affirm that the disability hasn't disappeared. Since Down syndrome is a permanent condition (the extra chromosome is in every cell in her body), you might not expect to have to prove her disability biannually. However, you would be wrong. Once after I was finished answering an official's phone call, my mother, who had listened to my side of the conversation, complimented me on my ability to remain polite. I replied that it was clear to me that they must know more about Down syndrome than I. I thought the extra chromosome was forever, but they clearly knew there was a cure! After a moment of silence, she laughed. Laughter makes many things go easier.

SUPPORT GROUPS

When Elaine was just an infant, I found a group of parents eager to create a support group in the District of Columbia. In this metropolitan area, Maryland, Virginia, and District of Columbia have different laws and agencies. It is important to have a support group in the jurisdiction where you live. Our group was sponsored by the National Children's Hospital and received initial funding from the March of Dimes. Although we were a Down syndrome parent group, we welcomed other families who had infants and children with disabilities. In many ways we were more alike than different in the issues we faced.

As a member of that group, I wrote a monthly newsletter. When Elaine was about to leave the Easter Seal's program, I had to find a nursery program that would accept my daughter. I visited a number of preschools and learned a great deal about which schools were truly inclusive and learned how many spaces each program had for the following year. I wrote an article about my research. The following month I received phone calls from parents who were seeking inclusive placements for their own children with special needs. I think some of the parents thought I was a placement agency!

When we moved to Maryland, I did not join the local Down syndrome group. By the time we arrived in upper Montgomery County, Maryland, the children were in elementary school and I was more interested in groups that would integrate both of them into the neighborhood. I was a Brownie Scout leader and helped in my son's Cub Scout troop. By high school, Special Olympics became our community. Today my daughter is involved in a number of activities and has several intersecting circles of friends.

In her teens, Elaine began attending an organization that matched her with a non-disabled individual for an hour of sports and games once a month. I needed to walk her to the door and pick her up but was asked not to stay. That was a huge moment for me. I began to understand that Elaine could function well without me. A friend with two sons with autism didn't believe this could possibly be the case with her sons, so on their first day with this group, she sat in the parking lot waiting for someone to find her and ask her to take her sons home. It didn't happen, and she was also startled that her sons had fun and were not anxious to leave when she came to pick them up. Finding out that children can function (at least for an hour) without you, forces a shift in perspective. The organization, Kids Enjoy Exercise Now (KEEN), provides an hour of activities and helps parents expand their understanding of their children's capabilities. After the first two years, Elaine was invited to another KEEN activity. When she reached her mid-twenties and definitely no longer fit the description of a "kid," she was invited to join an adult fitness group sponsored by KEEN but without one-on-one support. So she is able to continue with KEEN for an hour of exercise once a month at a local gym.

Elaine also joined an integrated percussion band in her late teens. She can't read music, but she learned to follow the conductor's directions and has enjoyed the weekly practices and concerts of this group. Part of the responsibilities of band members is to produce a solo performance at the end of a practice. These solos are followed by feedback from the other members of the band. My daughter has learned to plan and perform a solo and to listen to and give feedback. The interPLAY company Band has grown into an orchestra and practices in the education building next to Strathmore Music Center, a relatively new venue for music in the Washington, DC, area.

My daughter also belongs to an organization called Potomac Community Resources (PCR). PCR sponsors classes and activities in our suburban community. Once I was part of a parent group seeking to get a conversation class started. The parents found a professional willing to work with our young adults, and PCR—with its infrastructure—was able to secure a location for the class to meet, advertise the class, and collect the necessary fees. At about the same time, another group of parents were trying to get an activity started where their young adults could safely gather without the need of parental escorts. Once again, Potomac Community Resources (PCR) figured out how to make it happen. As the popularity of PCR grew, the idea of creating a similar organization in the upper part of our county led to the creation of the Upcounty Community Resources (UCR). Both PCR and UCR sponsor dances, activities, and classes.

In our county, Special Olympics is also an important source of activity and socialization. In addition to a full array of sports, there are holiday parties and other special events. So for my daughter there are many opportunities for meaningful activities as well as opportunities to meet others.

. . . .

HEAD OF HOUSEHOLD

By the time my children entered first grade, their father and I had divorced. Life as a single parent definitely has its challenges, but it means you just deal with things as they come. Actually, that is not true. You plan ahead and try to live one day at a time. You celebrate the small victories and deal with a problem, resolve it and then move on.

I had a taste of single parenting before the divorce. My husband was sent on an unaccompanied tour of duty before the twins were a year old. It was supposed to be a year but was extended to almost two years. That was a challenging time, but I knew that it was temporary. After the divorce it was different. The children flew out twice a year to visit their dad. At first, I wrote him about the children. Then as technology improved, I emailed him information about the children two or more times a month.

When they visited him, they had a good time. The flight to the Midwest was direct, and the two-hour journey helped them shift from one family to the other. I listened to their stories about their visit but never grilled them. I rejoiced that their stepmother and stepsisters embraced them. Although I was aware that my ex often came to the city on business, Louis and Elaine didn't know and thus were not hurt when he did not contact them. When they did see him, he was available to really engage with them. When he died unexpectedly, they received a call from their stepsister within an hour of his death. I will always be grateful that their stepmother considers them family and has continued to be a positive presence in their lives.

DREAMS

Parents have dreams for their children, but sometimes those are the parents' and not the child's hopes. I had dreams for Elaine and I was crushed when I heard the diagnosis of Down syndrome. In fact, I cried for months and did not find solace by visiting places that catered to young children with disabilities. I saw only what the children couldn't do. I wasn't ready to give up my dreams for Elaine because I didn't yet realize those dreams were mine, not hers.

Years later—long after I learned to see the abilities rather than the disabilities—I realized the truth behind my tears upon learning Elaine had an extra twenty-first chromosome. I was driving home after a particularly difficult parent conference. During the conference, my student stated that he really didn't want to study, didn't want my offers of help, and did not want to put the effort in to get a good grade. His parents were shocked and said that they had dreamed he would follow in his father's footsteps and become a lawyer. As I was thinking about the conference, it occurred to me that I, too, had wanted Elaine to be a super me—sort of my opportunity to relive my life. The tears shed so long ago were tears for a dream I lost; I was not crying because Elaine couldn't live out *her* dream. My student's parents would have to come to grips with the fact that their child couldn't live their dreams—something I tried to do when Elaine was an infant.

If dreams are going to be fulfilled, parents need to plan. As a single parent, I was motivated. I tried to imagine what a full life for my daughter would entail. A job, a place to live, friends and activities, ways to continue to learn, and church were all parts of the answer. The other part of a full life plan involves lawyers and financial planners. So, early in my life as a single parent, I talked to a lawyer, got financial advice and looked at my will, and did some estate planning. The plans for Elaine get reviewed in annual meetings. Every four to five years I review my legal and financial documents with professionals. Things change, and I want to leave a clear plan for my children, even though they are now adults.

• •

CHURCH

When Elaine was an infant, I asked our rector what we needed to do so that when she came of age she could take Communion. I wanted to start a process that would slowly prepare her for whatever she would need to do to be ready. I was startled when he told me that to receive Communion, Episcopalians only need to be baptized. Elaine had just been baptized, so I need not worry about her taking formal classes or passing any "test."

Our church community has always made whatever accommodations were necessary so that Elaine was and is fully included. At one time, children left the service before the sermon and returned before Communion when the peace is shared. The bulletin noted that this was for children between certain ages… until Elaine was older than the published age—and then the age specification just disappeared from the bulletin.

When Elaine was still very young, she wanted to be in the Christmas pageant. One of the teenagers in the parish asked if Elaine wanted to be a sheep, as she would be happy to be her shepherd. Elaine was thrilled to participate and we were deeply touched that members of our parish reached out to include her.

Today, Elaine carries a cross in the procession most Sundays. She chooses not to sit where acolytes sit near the altar, returning instead to sit with me in the front row. She chooses not to wear a robe. That is OK as well. She loves her role in the service and others expect to see her there.

When she had surgery to create a hip socket and was in a body cast at home for months, not only did folks from church come to bring her Communion, but she got cards almost daily. She loved receiving mail and it helped keep up her spirits.

The two of us now are responsible for selecting and then putting out the pastoral cards for the homebound or sick. These are signed following the service when people gather to socialize. We both understand how something so simple can have a powerful impact for those who are homebound.

FACING CRISES

When my husband returned from his long deployment in the Middle East, the children were toddlers, and we decided to drive him to work on the day he returned to his job in the Pentagon. Normally he took a bus, but we both wanted the children to know that their dad was going to an office, and not boarding a plane.

I returned to our home and walked in while an armed burglar was still in the house. To unlock the door, I had put Elaine down on the landing, turned the bolt lock, and then pushed the door open. Louis had rushed in. A man with a gun came between me and Louis. He did not see Elaine, still sitting just outside the door. He signaled for me to come in, but there was no way I would leave Elaine outside or Louis alone inside, so I shouted, "Help! I need help!"

In quick succession, the man with the gun ran past me, almost tripping over Elaine, as neighbors ran up the walk. Most of the neighbors knew my husband was on deployment and were unaware of his recent return. They ran to help a mom with two young children, then saw the man with the gun. The man ran down the sidewalk and jumped into a car. Other neighbors ran toward the house and helped in the immediate chaos.

The police were called first, but the second call was to a family in the playgroup. As I comforted both children, a playgroup mom arrived, scooped up both Louis and Elaine, and took them to play with her children. Much of the excitement was lost on Elaine, but Louis had nightmares for weeks until something happened that ended his night terrors.

The second trauma happened about two months later. The nanny took Louis and Elaine to visit friends one morning before I left for work. They were playing outside when a ball landed on a grate covering a window well. In our area of the world, houses have basements, and to let light in, there are window wells—basically areas dug out around the window and lined with something to keep the earth from filling the hole. This particular house had a grating over the window well. Louis and his friends scrambled to get the ball. The grate was rusted and gave way when Louis was on it. Louis plunged through the grate and landed on his arm. He fell eight feet and had cuts on his face from the rusty metal grate but missed going through the basement window.

At such a young age his bones were flexible, but the severity of the fall caused a bone in his arm to break. The doctors were more concerned by that than by the stitches required to close the gash on his forehead and over his lip. Once again the playgroup families sprang into action and took care of Elaine as the nanny, who had witnessed the accident, accompanied us as I drove to the clinic. Somehow the fall, scary as it was for Louis, didn't bring nightmares. But the nightmares about the man with the gun stopped.

About six months later, I was changing diapers early in the morning and discovered Elaine's was bright red. She did not appear to be bleeding. The urine-soaked diaper was red, not bloody, but I still went into a panic. It was a Saturday morning, so I woke up their dad and told him I was off with Elaine to the emergency room. I was there most of the day. Elaine didn't appear to be ill or suffering at all. I was questioned by social workers and doctors extensively.

During the course of reviewing the previous day's activities, I remembered that Elaine had come home from her program at Easter

Seal with a note that she had consumed lots of the finger paint. It turns out that red finger paint gets its color from beets, and the beets were the cause of her red urine and stool. I can report that most of the questions I had to answer had to do with other people interacting with Elaine the previous day. I apparently was never under suspicion of hurting my child.

FAIRNESS

Life isn't fair. This is something my son, Elaine's twin, learned early. On our first visit to Disney World, Louis noticed that another family had a child in a wheelchair (Elaine was in a handicap stroller) and they were standing at the back of a long line waiting for a ride. If you haven't been to Disney World, you may not know that the handicapped get to go to the head of the line.

Louis told the family, "You need to talk to my mom."

When I told them that they didn't need to wait in line, their response was, "That doesn't seem fair."

Louis was eight years old. He stood with his hands on his hips and said, "Surely you don't think life is fair!"

When the children were younger, we often stopped at a garage sale on the way home from church. Elaine was sometimes offered things for free, something that never happened for Louis. No one ever expected as much from Elaine as they did from Louis. Elaine had an easier time finding jobs than her brother. Louis was too skilled to qualify for jobs set aside for those with disabilities, yet his disability made it hard for him to land a job. In the end, things have worked out so that each has been able to live the life they want. It just took a bit longer than it did for the children and even the grandchildren of my brother and sisters.

PARENTING LOUIS

Early on, Louis provided a benchmark for what Elaine needed to work on. Rolling over, crawling, walking were all things Louis did first. When it became apparent that Louis also had special needs, therapists working with Elaine offered advice. Learning how to advocate for Elaine helped me learn how to do so for Louis. The first diagnosis for Louis was not Tourette's, but Attention Deficit Disorder. The doctor who diagnosed Louis told him he had something that made it hard for him to focus. Louis responded with relief, "You mean I am not retarded?" Apparently Louis thought he might have a milder form of whatever Elaine had.

He was given pills to help him pay attention, and for years he called them his focus pills. They did make a huge difference. Once he was at a friend's house and walked into the kitchen while the parents were in a heated discussion about the doctor's suggestion of a medication for their son. My son, true to both his age and his disability, interrupted and said he took pills to focus and it helped. The father phoned me to ask if it was true, and by the end of the phone call he said that perhaps he should investigate some more about the medication for his son.

When Louis was diagnosed with Tourette's, more pills were added to the mix. There is a whole list of medications that can and are prescribed to help individuals deal with the symptoms. It took a while to find the combination that worked for Louis. The primary physician and orthopedic surgeon we had in the military retired the same year that Louis and Elaine no longer qualified for military medicine. We shifted to an HMO I could access through my employer.

During the first visit, I informed the doctor that Louis had prescriptions that needed to be refilled. The doctor looked at the names of the medications and asked, "What idiot would prescribe these two together?" I responded with the doctor's name and the immediate response was, "Oh, the doctor we refer all our special-needs kids to!" The prescriptions were filled.

Louis doesn't look disabled, and in many ways that made it doubly difficult for him in school. Louis often was accused of not paying attention, when, in fact he was, but his behaviors suggested otherwise. His behaviors (avoiding eye contract, looking into the distance rather than the chalkboard) are in mix of things that are characteristic of Tourette's syndrome. His doctor told me that if I could get Louis through school with his confidence intact, he would be fine.

Wonderful teachers along the way helped, and lots of patience also helped, but it is hard having a disability when you do not look like you have a disability.

The diagnosis of Tourette's was devastating for me. The doctor was called in to consult with us at the clinic. She walked into the room, looked at Louis, turned, and said, "Tourette's," as she left the room. I was clueless. When our primary physician returned, he helped me understand what the term meant and also explained that the next evening a physician very knowledgeable about the syndrome was speaking locally.

I attended the meeting. That doctor described the symptoms of the condition—describing my son perfectly—and he had yet to meet him! At the break, I shamelessly approached him. He asked me if I would consent to Louis being part of a research project. That meant Louis would receive a stipend, and I would be able to meet with the doctor and get his take on the appropriate medication and recommended next steps. What a blessing that was! Thus began my education about my son's disability. It also was the first time Louis was able to talk with someone knowledgeable about what was going on in his mind.

We could see the tics and other visible behaviors. Louis tended to run from one side of a room to another, using his hands to push off one wall and then the next. Thank heavens we had a split foyer home, so his running was on the ground floor. The oil from his hands made short work of any paint on the walls, but it was a way for him to work out the tics. I knew that he didn't pick up social cues and so I taught him it was important to look people in the eye when speaking to them. I knew about the tics I could see, but I was shocked to hear the doctor talk about his internal tics. Louis apparently had a string of nonsense words he had to say to himself when processing new thoughts. Because he had difficulty printing and never has mastered cursive writing, he relies on active listening when in the classroom. Imagine how difficult it must be to listen when you have to deal with internal "tics."

Tics generally associated with Tourette's are swearing. Louis never did that. In fact, his most annoying tic for years was sniffing. He didn't have a cold or allergies. It was a tic. Tics are similar to an itch that demands a response. However, when you scratch an itch it just makes the impulse worse, and so it is with tics. Tics tend to worsen when under stress or feeling anxious. School definitely brought out the worst tics. In Louis's case, he kept most of it under control (other than the sniffing) until he got home. When things aren't stressful, the tics seem to diminish and almost disappear.

Tics can and do change. Once I was in an important meeting at school and was pulled out to talk to the nurse at Louis's school. Louis's tic of choice was to crack his neck. Apparently, he was stuck in a painful position and they wanted me to pick him up. Because I could not leave immediately to pick him up, I asked the nurse to treat his neck with ice packs and, if possible, give him an aspirin. I also asked the nurse to tell him while he waited for me to think of another tic to replace cracking his neck! Years later, the surgeon who did my back surgery heard this story about my son and said, "Wow, most people don't know that tics can change." Louis knows, and says it takes mental discipline to do it.

Louis was often the target of bullies and always ended up frustrating some of his teachers. He certainly was no fun in the evening when he struggled with homework assignments. The biggest challenge for him in terms of homework was putting his thoughts on paper—literally printing the letters. For a while, I took dictation and printed for him, but that led to lots of angry shouting from Louis because he didn't think I was actually taking down his words as he said them. The solution was an early version of a computer program called Dramatically Speaking. Louis spoke to the computer, the computer printed what he said, and Louis was able to independently do his homework.

Elementary, middle, and high school all presented challenges for him. Our school district did a great job with all sorts of learning disabilities. If students were shapes, our school district could teach circles, squares, rectangles, and triangles. But my son was a trapezoid. I just got so tired of teachers trying to shave down his sides to fit him into one of the shapes they liked to teach. Once he graduated from high school and had greater flexibility in his course of study, he did well.

When Louis was in college, he received a letter informing him that he had earned an award. I took time off from work to go to the ceremony. I had to remind my son to dress appropriately. As a result, at the ceremony he was one of a very few students who didn't look as if he had just rolled out of bed. His friends greeted me enthusiastically, "Hi Louis's Mom," and then seemed to realize that wasn't quite right. In whispered tones, they asked Louis about his last name, and then greeted me more formally.

After the ceremony, Louis and his friends made a beeline to the refreshment table, but I stood in line, waiting to speak to the Dean of the College. The woman behind me in line sought me out later and commented that she now understood why her son loved this college . . . just like her son who avoided eye contact, the Dean also avoided eye contact. I realized at that point that there were many at the college (including the faculty) who had disabilities somewhat like my son's. One of life's blessings is finding a community that understands and accepts individuals with disabilities, yet maintains high standards.

Louis has always been a terrific advocate for Elaine. Long before she had language skills, she developed a sign language of sorts. We all understood it, but Louis was the one who put it into words. Eventually, we did learn American Sign Language, but Louis—from the first— informed a caregiver or nurse what Elaine meant when she used one of her signs. Louis has continued to advocate and at times translate for Elaine. When she was hospitalized in her twenties for severe pain in her abdominal area, he sat with her during the one morning I had to go to work. He made certain the medical team understood that she had a high tolerance for pain and that they should take her pain seriously.

Louis is respectful and would never do for Elaine what she can do for herself. He will assist when assistance is needed, but is accepting of differences. It is a skill that makes him wonderful with the elderly and the disabled. One time, we were at an event when we mistakenly took someone else's handicap stroller and not our own. When we went to return the stroller and retrieve ours, we found ourselves in a home with a child who had multiple handicaps. We were ushered into the kitchen where everyone was chatting, everyone that is, except the young man with the disability. The young man was on a couch in another room, with a communication board in front of him. He saw us and waved his arms frantically. Louis went to the couch and joined him. After twenty minutes, the parents asked where Louis was. When they learned he was with their son, they asked him what he was doing. Louis said that the two of them had interesting things to "talk about." Their son nodded in agreement. The parents were stunned. I wasn't. That was just Louis being Louis.

By the age of ten, Louis figured out that he would always be involved in some way in Elaine's life. He was visiting his father when he told him that "Mom is getting on in years, and I will need to step up to the plate." His father was startled and told me about the conversation.

When Louis returned home, I did my best to reassure Louis that he can live his own life and will never need to be the primary support or caregiver for his sister. However, he has intentionally selected jobs that keep him in our metropolitan area. He says he hopes to be only a phone call away, should she need something. He is an important part of her community of support.

AN INDIVIDUAL FIRST, NOT A DISABILITY

People with disabilities are first and foremost individuals. They prefer to be seen for their capabilities rather than their disabilities. Louis and I have always said Elaine is just like everyone else, only more so. Her extra chromosome seems to make her just that much more stubborn or that much more gregarious. My daughter, to coin the phrase used by the National Down Syndrome Congress (NDSC), is more alike than different. More importantly, while she knows she has Down syndrome (she is proud to attend the annual convention of the National Down Syndrome Congress), she would never describe herself as someone with a disability or even with Down syndrome. She thinks she is perfect as she is.

When my daughter was a child, I was often praised for being calm when it was clear to everyone she was doing something particularly embarrassing. Usually, I did not deserve the praise because they were referring to someone else's child, not my daughter. I wish others would recognize that people with Down syndrome have an extra chromosome in common but do not look alike!

In the early days, I found the term mongoloid offensive. Now I just figure the individual is stuck in the 1950s and has limited knowledge. I also don't like the term retarded as it is currently used. Mostly people use the term as slang for stupid. Certainly that was my experience when working in a public high school. If a student in my class used the word, I would explain that the term actually meant the development of the brain was delayed and was not a synonym for stupid. I then explained that if they met my daughter and observed how she almost always put forth her best effort, they would never insult her by using the term when they wanted to call out a classmate for a mistake or a dumb move. I told them if someone did something stupid, use the correct word, not a word that hurts those who face multiple challenges. My students stopped using retard and retarded but others, including members of the faculty, did not.

It still grates my nerves when I hear the term Down's syndrome or Downs (as in the expression, "I know someone with Downs"). Years ago the organizations supporting people with Down syndrome argued that Dr. Down may have discovered the syndrome, but he does not own it. There is only one "s" in Down syndrome.

When Elaine attended her first NDSC convention as a self-advocate, she was pleased to find a room filled with people somewhat like her. For her, it was an instant community. That was when I realized that by fully integrating her, she had really never spent time with others with Down syndrome. We now make a point of attending the annual NDSC convention every year. I enjoy my conference and she attends the one designed by and for self-advocates.

A WORK IN PROGRESS

While we are all works in progress, sometimes it seems that someone with discernible disabilities is deemed fair game for comments designed to improve or educate. These comments suggest that people with developmental delays are projects that need fixing. In the case of my daughter, much of the attempted correction goes right over her head, but I hear it and it hurts.

Sometimes the words of wisdom are mean-spirited. Other times, the suggestions may be good but are delivered in a way that causes, rather than solves, problems. Usually it is handed out by folks who are totally clueless about my daughter's abilities.

When Elaine was about nine years old, her way of complaining about some perceived injustice (which I may or may not have been complicit in), would be to say, "Mommy is a bad mom." A friend, hearing this, decided to shift her tone and taught her a little song and dance with a rumba beat. Instead of *stating* I was a bad mom, she would *sing*, "Mommy is a bad mom," and do her little dance and giggle. She could be counted on to do this in the line at the grocery store, at church, and at various events. Just as predictably, strangers, family, and friends would all knock themselves out telling her that her mommy was a good mom. It took years to break that habit, particularly as it got her the attention she craved. Oh, how I wish I had been able to stop that before it started, because even if it takes a lot of time to teach Elaine something, it takes longer for her to break a bad habit.

Sometimes the intervention on Elaine's behalf can be dangerous. We were at the zoo when Elaine and her brother were seven years old. Elaine loved to run. She tended to sprint for a couple of yards and then stop and drop. She was too big for a stroller and I had not yet discovered handicapped strollers. I was using a harness on her, holding both the tether and her hand, while her brother held my other hand. That day we had just crossed the road from the parking lot, when a stranger walked right up to me and yelled, "She's not a dog!" I shifted my focus from Elaine for just a moment. Elaine jerked hard and ran away with the tether of the harness dragging behind her. I dashed after her and caught up with her just as she made it to the road. That incident is an example of stranger danger that many children typically don't encounter. Not long after that I purchased a stroller for the handicapped that could support her weight and, more importantly, had seat belts that she was unable to unlatch.

As Elaine has matured, she has acquired skills that help her become more self-reliant. She also has picked up new habits that are challenging. Currently she likes to pull on threads. Typically, they are threads in a waistband, but they could also be a seam. She pulls, the threads unravel, and soon there is a gap in a seam or a waistband that is no longer connected to the pants! Thank heavens for sewing machines. Her counselor works with Elaine to inspect clothing periodically to ensure what she puts on is in one piece.

In her early teens, Elaine chewed and picked at the nails on her fingers and toes. Sometimes the fingers and toes were raw and bloody. We tried painting the nails with something that was supposed to taste bad, but it did not deter her. She has beautiful nails now. The solution came from a visit to St. Louis. Her wonderful stepmother took her to a nail salon for a manicure and pedicure. Now manicures and pedicures are part of her routine. The days of picking at her nails are long past.

• •

There are still challenging behaviors. Food, particularly sweet and/or salty items, is a constant temptation. Despite best intentions, it is tough to control. Elaine does avoid foods with gluten, but otherwise it is tough controlling her impulses. Long before Elaine moved into her own place, we had stopped bringing snack foods, sodas, sweets, and ice cream into the house. One of the conditions of being her roommate was the promise not to bring those temptations into the condo, unless they were kept in the roommate's bedroom. Despite promises and constant reminders, her first roommate brought in large containers of ice cream. Bringing ice cream into her condo is like putting alcohol in front of an alcoholic. Elaine continued to gain weight. In the first year and a half living in her own place, she gained about twenty-five pounds—she was already twenty pounds overweight to start.

Exercise is part of her regular routine, but that has not had a noticeable impact on reducing her weight. What has worked is portion control. We prepare five days of meals (breakfast, lunch, and dinner) at a time. The meals are gluten free, low calorie, and balanced nutritionally. And they are meals she likes. She puts them into containers that have dividers (imagine the containers once used for TV dinners) that are both freezer and microwave safe. The meals are frozen, and when she is ready to eat, she selects the meal she wants and puts it into the microwave. The only things in the refrigerator are milk and her homemade applesauce (no sugar). The freezer compartment, however, is packed with her containers. Four months on this regime led to a loss of twenty pounds and she continues to lose weight, though more slowly at this point. Happily, her new roommate does not bring in foods that tempt Elaine to "cheat."

STUBBORNNESS OR PERSISTENCE?

Stubbornness is both her strength and her weakness. There is a right way and a wrong way. To take the edge off the battles, we worked from the start to introduce alternate ways of doing things. We varied times we left for routine events and we also varied the routes. This meant she learned from an early age that there were two, or perhaps three, ways we might do things. Mostly this worked. But we did not vary her bedtime, and I still recall the dinner party when she announced to my guests as the hour approached 9:00 p.m., "It is time for you to go home and go to bed!"

Stubbornness is also persistence. Persistence got her to finally learn how to operate a combination lock on her high school locker; it resulted in her ability to read at the age of twenty-eight after years of struggling; and it accounts for most of her successes. Elaine wanted to use the monkey bars on the elementary school playground, but she couldn't master the hand-to-hand motion necessary to swing across the span. Her solution was to climb up over the bars and belly-crawl across the top. The playground aides were beside themselves with worry. Whenever Elaine managed to, she would repeat the same thing over and over. Eventually she did master the monkey bars. She just stuck with it. The trick is to use the trait of persistence without getting trapped by the stubbornness.

SENSE OF TIME

Elaine's sense of time is unique and shared by others with disabilities. To her, something that happened years ago can seem fresh, as if it just happened. For example, even though her grandfather died over twenty years ago, something can trigger the memory, and his death becomes so fresh that she gets weepy. People who do not know her believe the death just occurred. This trait is explained with humor by one of the doctors who operates a Down syndrome clinic in the Midwest.

The good news is that happy memories are as easily recalled as sad ones. Something can trigger a memory and she will begin chuckling and then laughing. We won't quite understand the reason until she catches her breath and explains.

MOOD SHIFTING

Getting unstuck. Elaine can get in a snit, and often she goes to her room to calm herself down—a good strategy if you think about it. However, if we don't have the luxury of time for her to calm down, I have found that Elaine *loves* to have her hair washed. When she is upset and being difficult, I ask if she wants to have her hair washed. She then appears with a towel around her neck, shampoo in her hand, and goes to the kitchen sink where I wash her hair and she typically belts out her version of "I'm Going to Wash That Man Right out of My Hair." It is definitely a mood shifter for her. It has been my experience that all of us respond well to a shift in focus when we are angry or upset.

SECRETS

Elaine isn't great at keeping secrets. It isn't that she is childlike; it is more that she gets so excited that she has something for you, or possibly knows of a special event that will please you. Others with disabilities often blurt out a secret because they simply don't see it as something to be hidden. Once someone in the special-needs community has learned that it's my birthday, there is no point in keeping it secret. The information is widely shared, as is my age. One of the fun things about some of my daughter's friends is their ability to tell me the day of the week when I was born and the day of the week of next year's birthday. If it is really important to keep a particular secret, we talk with Elaine and tell her why it is important that she not share the information. If we explain it in terms of hurting feelings or ruining a surprise, she "gets it" and won't share the information.

SOCIAL IQ

Elaine's academic IQ isn't very high, but she definitely has a high social IQ. She senses when someone is feeling sad and will try to cheer them up. She is quick with praise, "You are handsome; you are so pretty; your baby is so cute." She loves to remember people on their birthdays with a card and present.

We did need to temper her outgoingness. We taught her to greet people with a handshake, reserving hugs for those whom we knew well. In fact, one of the "rules" for the volunteers in the bowling program I managed for Special Olympics is not to assume the athletes want to be hugged. If an athlete knows you and initiates a hug, hug back. But just as you would not hug a stranger, do not assume the athlete wants to be touched or hugged.

One of the Resource Counselors assigned to work with my daughter arrived at our home for an initial meeting with her. When my daughter put her hand out to shake, the woman pulled her into a bear hug—very inappropriate. In the ensuing conversation, it was clear she saw my daughter as a child and not as a young adult. In the musical chairs that so often happens in the world of special needs, that individual was promoted to another position before a second meeting... thank heavens!

To celebrate her twenty-first birthday, we flew to the Bahamas. While boarding the plane, Elaine walked down the aisle to our seat complimenting everyone on their good looks. As a result, these folks were not strangers for long. When we walked to the pool the second day of the trip, I noticed that virtually every chair had a towel on it. I need not have worried about finding a place to settle as people called out to "Elaine's Mom" and offered us chairs, umbrellas, etc. They all remembered Elaine.

In the evening when we walked around the square, we noticed a band setting up. As soon as the music started, Elaine was out in front of the band dancing and waving her arms trying to get others to join her. Some of the college students who had been on the plane did join her, and assured me that they would watch out for Elaine in the crowded dance area. They also promised to dance Elaine over to me before they left for dinner. Elaine had a great time and was ready to leave when they returned her to me.

Elaine still loves to dance and is not at all shy about dancing on her own without a partner. At the party celebrating my retirement, Elaine was on the dance floor as soon as the music started. In no time at all, others got up to join her. A guest sitting at our table announced earlier in the evening she had never danced. However, when she saw Elaine dancing alone, she got up and joined her. She later told me, "If Elaine can do it, so can I!" Elaine definitely made it easy for her and for others to join in. It helps that as she dances, Elaine waves her hands signaling for others to join her.

Elaine and her friends are very accepting of others with disabilities. Some of Elaine's friends do not look like they have a disability; others do, but they all accept each other. At a dance, folks may dance by themselves, with a partner, with a group, or just around a friend in a wheelchair so he or she feels included. Attending a dance with Elaine and her friends is a lesson in inclusion as well as a lot of fun.

Elaine's social awareness means she can pick up on tension easily. If someone is upset with another person, Elaine senses it and gets moody herself. Yet, in spite of this sensitivity, she has had to be taught social and communication boundaries. The most effective tool we found is called the Circles Curriculum. The program was introduced to her slowly and it took lots of role- playing and practice, but she did learn the difference between family, friends, acquaintances, and

· ·

strangers. We support Elaine by periodically reviewing the lessons in that curriculum. She appears to understand when someone moves from one circle to another because she arranges the framed pictures in her room according to her sense of close friends and/or family versus those she is no longer emotionally close to.

DATING AND MARRIAGE

Many of Elaine's friends date and are in committed relationships. Some have married—that is, they say they are married, but due to the desire to remain eligible for the funding that provides needed supports, they had a ceremony and reception but did not legally wed. These relationships take commitment of the young couple but also involve the support of the families who love them.

My daughter wants to get married. She says so. It has been on her list of goals posted on her bedroom door for a long time. What she really means is she wants a wedding—a party with friends, food, and dancing—where *she* is the center of attention. She doesn't really want a husband.

How do I know this? Elaine has no real sense of loyalty. She has a boyfriend, but if he isn't around, she gravitates to the cutest boy in the room. Also, her current desire is to marry Prince Eric or Prince Ali (characters in Disney movies). Until she demonstrates a level of commitment to another, she isn't ready to be married. However, when she does, and he does, I will do what I can to support them both.

CONCEPTUALIZATION AND ANTICIPATION

When Elaine was an infant, we were told that she would stop learning at the age of seven and that she would never be able to conceptualize or anticipate. How wrong they were! For a long time, Elaine wrote out lists of people she planned to invite to her next birthday party (often within hours of the end of the current year's party) and showed her displeasure with someone by cutting that individual from her list. In fact, I have never met anyone with a developmental disability for whom a birthday wasn't a big occasion that was eagerly anticipated.

Elaine has always loved stories with a heroine. Cinderella, Sleeping Beauty, Belle in Beauty and the Beast, the Little Mermaid, and the sisters in Frozen are among her favorites. Currently she enjoys copying the stories in her neat printing and inserting her name where Cinderella, Sleeping Beauty, or any other heroine's name should be. She staples the pages into a book and has assembled quite a collection. Wishful thinking? Or do these books reflect her ability to conceptualize?

Like most people, Elaine likes to win. Unlike most people, Elaine signs up on all sorts of lists, and often she "wins" something. We "won" a collapsible wheelchair once because she signed a list at a fair. Sometimes her signature commits me to things, obligations that I learn about long after she has put pen to paper.

One Saturday I got a call from a member of our church giving me a head count. When I asked what this was for, she told me that I had signed up for refreshments. I told her I had no idea I had done so. I asked if the name was signed in a scrawl or printed neatly. The neat printing was Elaine's! This is an example of when Elaine really didn't understand the commitment behind her signature.

SELF-TALK

Elaine has conversations with herself. Her conversations aren't like mine, which tend to be just talking out loud. Elaine actually has an exchange with herself. For example, if she is trying to make a decision, she typically creates a persona to talk to. She says something in one voice and then moves to a different place in the room, and in a different voice responds. This exchange may go on for a while until she reaches a decision.

While visiting my sister, she had a conversation with herself that my sister could hear through the bathroom door. My sister was convinced someone was in the room with her. She even checked the room after Elaine walked out! One of the wise doctors who works in a Down syndrome clinic advises his patients to conduct these conversations with a cell phone held to their ear or, as Elaine did, behind closed doors!

MAKE BELIEVE

It is fun to go to Disney World with someone who believes. Elaine believes totally that the mouse with the big ears and big feet is Mickey and that, like all of the other costumed characters, he is real. She is not the only one, either! A few years ago, the NDSC held a conference on a Disney property. Cinderella was in the registration area. A line of young people was waiting to have their picture taken with her. One toddler crawled over and lifted her skirt, much to his parents' horror. Once he saw the glass slipper, he dropped the skirt and scooted back into the line. Cinderella leaned down and spoke to the child as his parents looked at those of us standing nearby—we knew he was just checking to see if she was the "real deal," and happily she was.

Elaine used to love to have her picture taken with Santa. It never confused her to see Santas all over town because in her eyes Christmas is when we celebrate the birth of Jesus, presents are exchanged between families and friends, and you take your picture with Santa. One time, a "Santa" asked her what she wanted from Santa for Christmas, and even though she wasn't particularly articulate, she told the startled Santa that Mom already got her presents.

Another Santa story involved an event at the National Cathedral during Advent. Elaine had participated in an activity where she made a small wreath, heard a story, and then had an opportunity to see St Nicholas greet the children. Elaine, in a handicapped stroller pushed by her brother, waited for the crowd to clear so she could actually see

St Nick. When most of the crowd had moved on to another activity, her brother pushed her forward and she gave St Nick her handmade wreath. To Elaine, he was not someone impersonating St Nicholas; he *was* St. Nick. Apparently, her act of giving was the subject of the homily during the service the next morning at the Cathedral. We heard about it because a member of our parish attended and figured that, based on the description, it had to be Elaine.

For years, Elaine has loved the music and the story of *The Phantom of the Opera*. She identifies with the Phantom, whom she sees as the underdog because he is disfigured. She has a strong desire to help people she feels are treated poorly because of a physical or cognitive handicap. I suspect she see it as an issue of standing together to face the world.

BEING INDEPENDENT VERSUS BEING RESPONSIBLE

When she turned twenty-one, Elaine liked to state she was independent. She used her claim of "independence" as an explanation for why she did not comply with rules or fulfill obligations at her job. Actually, when Elaine is corrected or even reminded about something, her stock response is, "I know," or "it's my day," phrases that are best translated as "leave me alone," or less politely, "bug off."

It has taken a lot of patience and much discussion to help her understand that being independent requires taking responsibility for her actions. For several years this issue has been the subject of Individual Plans (these replace the IEPs during her school years).

SELF-CONFIDENCE

Elaine can be shy, but generally she exudes self-confidence. When the rector of our church was "new," he was touched that Elaine always took the time to say hello when she entered the building and always told him when she was leaving. He did not realize that she was actually telling him he could start because she had arrived and that he could "shut it down" because she was leaving.

Years ago, I was in the room with a number of people when her boyfriend at the time insulted her in front of everyone in the room. I was shocked and upset for her, but she amazed me and everyone in the room with her response. Elaine looked the young man in the eye and said, "You have no reason to be mean to me." There was a collective sigh of relief in the room and a collective, "Way to go, Elaine." Perhaps that extra chromosome comes with a heavy dose of confidence?

EXERCISE AND SPORTS

In St Louis, the public swimming pools are huge and the shallow end is relatively deep. At well under four feet, Elaine couldn't stand in the shallow end, and, because being able to swim across the pool was a prerequisite to jumping off the diving board, she was motivated to learn. Her stroke wasn't recognizable and she mostly swam under the surface of the water bobbing up for air, but she passed the test and was able to join her friends on the diving board.

When we returned to Maryland a year later, she swam the length of the pool in a similar fashion in an effort to persuade the lifeguards to let her jump from the low diving board. This time she didn't pass. They didn't like her breathing. Several parents challenged the lifeguards, pointing out that their children touched bottom, essentially cheating, while Elaine made it across mostly under the surface of the water entirely on her own without touching the bottom.

Eventually, the lifeguards were persuaded and Elaine could join her friends and jump from the board. That experience motivated me to get someone to work with her to improve her swimming technique. She is now on a Special Olympic swim team. She isn't fast, but she is steady and has a recognizable stroke.

Several years ago, she went to a pool with her aunt. My sister was worried that Elaine would disrupt lap swimmers, and put her in an empty lane. She reported that members of swim teams came and swam laps in the lane next to Elaine, and once they were done with their laps, they left. Elaine, however, continued to swim for two hours. When she was done, she got out of the pool and announced it was time to go home. My sister was amazed that Elaine outlasted the teams and had no interest in playing in the pool. I suspect that it was just the routine Elaine was used to. In Elaine's experience, one goes to pools to swims laps.

Elaine swims, sails, and bowls with Special Olympics. She also goes to a gym. For a while she worked with a personal trainer. She loved it, but it was expensive so we were not able to sustain it. She loves the Zumba class at the gym and has no hesitation at all when asked to come to the front of the class and help lead. She also has a stationary bike in her condo that she uses daily.

A favorite form of exercise for Elaine is dancing. She used to dance until the last song, but although she still dances as soon as the music starts, an hour and a half after nonstop dancing, she often tells me that it is time to go home. Now that she is losing weight, I hope that she will have more energy.

A PICTURE IS WORTH A THOUSAND WORDS

Taking a chapter from Vanna White on TV who routinely uses "visual aids," we learned the value of pictures and other visuals. Elaine talked in phrases for a long time. Because it was often difficult to really understand what she was trying to communicate, we sent her to family events and other activities with a photo album full of pictures of her engaged in activities. This was particularly helpful when she visited her father, because it helped fill in the gaps. Everyone understands phrases when linked to pictures. She was able to share her experiences, and as a strategy, it works.

An important visual aid is a calendar. We use calendars for conveying information. If plans have to be changed, the calendar is changed (early on this was done without Elaine seeing it). So when Elaine insisted that we had to do or go somewhere, she was referred to her calendar and saw that, no, the event was scheduled for another time. Now, Elaine adds things to—and makes changes on—her own calendar. A calendar is a way for her to have a clear idea of the activities of her day, the week, and the month.

Now that she is on her own, the visuals have increased. She has a chart on the inside of the front door listing the times she has to leave each morning. She has two different jobs, and three different departure times Monday through Friday. It is a problem if she leaves too early or too late. The chart works.

Also, she needs help determining appropriate outerwear. We have a chart with pictures of her in different outerwear, reminding her of what to wear when it is cold and rainy, hot and rainy, snowing, etc. There is a chart next to her first-aid kit and a chart of what to do in emergencies, along with contact numbers by her home phone.

UNDERSTANDING AND BEING UNDERSTOOD.

Elaine and others with developmental delays tend to be literal, very literal. Elaine was in a three- month residential program designed to help with the transition out of high school. She lasted one month. There were two complaints about her. The first complaint was that she had horrible hygiene. I asked for specifics. They told me they asked her in class if she showered and she said no. I then asked them if they had actually checked her shower and her towels. They did, and they were puzzled why she would say no. Proof of her using the shower was apparent, and when an older and wiser supervisor looked at Elaine and her clean hair and body, she knew Elaine had showered. I said that when they asked her if she showered, she heard, "Are you in the shower?" As Elaine was in class and not in the shower, her response naturally was no.

The second complaint was Elaine's behavior when her request to change her roommate did not result in a desired outcome. Elaine moved her roommate's things out, carefully placing them in the closet and drawers of another room, and moved the possessions of a girl she wanted to room with into her room with the same care. She even changed the name tags on the doors.

Clearly, she should not have done this, and this spelled the end of her participation in the program. It does demonstrate, however, her wish to be understood when her oral communication missed the mark.

Another communication issue for Elaine is one that is shared by others in her circle of friends. When she is asked to make a choice—for example, *do you want to go with me to the store*; her response may reflect something other than a simple yes or no. If she is engaged in something interesting, her initial response may be, no, but she may actually mean, *no, not yet*.

For example, on a visit to a relative, Elaine was watching a video when asked if she wanted to go swimming. She said no. The relative was disappointed but then surprised when twenty minutes later Elaine appeared with her suit on and her towel over her shoulder. What happened? Elaine said no, meaning I don't want to go *now*, not really meaning she didn't want to go at all. This is either a case of taking things literally or it is a processing problem, but it happens to others with developmental delays. The lesson here is to ask the question clearly and do some checking to learn if "no" really means "no" or just "not right at the moment."

PRONUNCIATION OR COMMUNICATION?

Elaine had significant delays in her speech. She spoke words, then phrases. And much, much later she began to speak in sentences. By high school, it was clear she needed to learn how to communicate more effectively. She had years of speech therapy—initially privately and then through public schools—but what really helped her communicate were classes and workshops where the goal was communication, not pronunciation. In fact, one year at the annual IEP meeting I was told quite clearly that it was not realistic to expect Elaine to be more articulate. That statement prompted me focus my efforts. I signed Elaine up for a speech-making class at our community college. It was offered as a noncredit course for those with developmental disabilities. Over the course of a semester, she learned to write and say a five-sentence speech. She gained confidence in the class as she rehearsed her speech, and her articulation improved.

When Elaine had the opportunity to apply to transition programs housed outside the high school, the benefits of being engaged with peers in her community paid off. The screening process for Elaine involved a visit to the program, while the director and teachers watched her interaction with the other participants. Elaine was still speaking in phrases and was not always articulate. However, the students in the room were friends from Special Olympics. They knew her, understood her, and she spent a happy two hours engaged in the activities. Elaine got in the program because of those relationships more than her articulation.

. . . .

The year she entered the transition program she was selected for a Special Olympics- Gallup Organization program that significantly improved her communication skills. Matched with a mentor from Gallup, she traveled each month by metro from our suburban community to a class held at the Gallup headquarters in downtown DC. She developed a speech about herself and then practiced saying it. At the graduation, she delivered it as part of the ceremony. She used cue cards during the speech. She began, stumbled, went back to the beginning, and delivered a speech that was articulate and touching.

At that point, she was comfortable on stage and interested in accepting an invitation to be a panelist at the National Down Syndrome Congress annual conference. She practiced for almost a year before she gave her panel presentation. She used visuals (at the time overheads) to support her comments, and no doubt that helped both her and the audience. But she actually conveyed her message clearly to the 250 self-advocates in the audience. Elaine rose to the challenge.

Once she was articulate, we needed to work on conversational skills, because she tended to "broadcast" rather than engage in the back and forth of conversation. For several years she has been in a conversation class facilitated by a speech therapist. This class is all about initiating conversation and engaging with others and has helped her communicate more effectively. She has learned to take turns in conversation and to ask follow-up questions. There is a pattern to the conversational exchange that she learns in class. "How was your weekend?" is the opener and she follows up with, "And what did you do next?"

Now when she speaks in a public gathering, it typically meets the two "A's": articulate and appropriate.

TECHNOLOGICAL AIDS TO COMMUNICATION

Communication boards were first introduced when Elaine began speech therapy. She moved on to computer programs that pronounced words as she spelled them and read a sentence once a period was added. The robotic voice helped her hear all parts of the word. Elaine was at one time able to access the Internet. That access ended because she was unable to use it appropriately. She tried to buy wedding gowns and diamond rings, continually! As a result, she did not have a smart phone until recently. Although she has a tablet, she is unaware that when her brother loads movies, games, and puzzles, he uses her tablet to access the Internet.

My daughter moved into her own place in October 2014. She has matured and become more independent with that move. However, when she first moved into her own place, she did not answer either the landline or her cell phone. It took three months, but I finally figured out that this was a processing problem. I learned to call, identify myself when the answering machine kicked in, call again, and by the third call she would pick up. Why? I think she noticed the phone ringing, but was occupied with something that she wanted to finish. The second time the phone rang, she figured she probably needed to answer it, and by the third time the phone rang, she acted and picked up the phone.

Six months later she began to pick up as soon as she identified my voice on the answering machine. In fact, she displayed just how much she understood the skill of telephone communication when the paratransit van failed to pick her up to take her to one of her jobs, and she called her boss to let him know she would be late. She also phoned her job coach. She didn't call me, but the job coach did, and I got her to work. I asked her to call me, and the next day she did call to let me know she had been picked up and was in the van. She continues to answer on the first or second ring and that is progress. However, this remains a work in progress.

TRUTHFULNESS

In general, my daughter tells the truth. In high school, elated that she was taking a class at the local community college, she bragged to her classmates. Her teachers corrected her and let me know that Elaine was telling lies. The community college had Challenge Classes (noncredit) for individuals with disabilities, but they were still in their early years so not widely known. Elaine's teachers didn't back down until I offered to show them the receipt for the tuition I had paid.

It has been my experience that most people do tell the truth if asked questions in a way that doesn't instantly make them defensive. In the course of managing a large program for Special Olympics, it is not unusual for one athlete to complain about another. If I can get the parents to step back, I can generally find a resolution satisfactory to all. If I listen carefully and ask follow-up questions, generally it isn't hard to discover what the problem is. Thanking the athletes for seeking help rather than getting into an argument helps. I have also learned that pointing out that the problem may be linked to an athlete's disability helps. Generally, the athlete with the complaint tells me, "oh, I understand disability," and we move on to working on a solution.

HYGIENE

Teaching girls about menstruation is awkward anyway but takes more effort when they have developmental delays. Amazingly, I found that simply talking to my daughter about her becoming a woman and listening to and responding to her questions worked. All the books with diagrams I purchased or borrowed from the public library made no sense to her. Happily, our discussions did. Because she is a swimmer, I also talked to her about tampons and how to insert them. I bought the thinnest possible ones on the market at the time, but it really wasn't as big a deal as I feared. She never really could anticipate (even with calendars) when her cycle might start, so she always carries supplies in her purse or fanny pack. This turned out to be important several years later when a young woman on the swim team was about to compete when it became clear to her coaches that her cycle had begun. I was asked by the male coach to help. What happened next was really educational.

First, the young woman was upset by her own blood and needed help to calm down. Second, it turned out that she only used pads. With pads, she would need to get dressed and would be able to cheer for her team, but she could not get back into the pool. She wanted to compete. So my task was to explain what a tampon was and how to insert it. It turns out that she thought it was dirty to touch herself "down there" and it took more calming and quiet discussion. I assured her that bodily fluids are normal and nothing to be afraid of, and that just like every time one uses the toilet, it is important to wash your hands afterwards. After she went through four of the five tampons from my daughter's stash, I told her that this was the last one, and if it went in the toilet, she was using a pad, getting dressed, and sitting in the bleachers. It went in; she washed her hands and went on to compete. However, because of the howling from the young woman (eew! oh no! eek! ahh! nooo!), at one point an adult using another stall in the bathroom asked me if I was assisting in a birth.

Later that morning, the mother of the young woman arrived, learned of what had transpired and confronted me. She was very upset and told me that I had no right to force her daughter to use a tampon. My response was that her daughter had been given a choice and elected to use a tampon and compete. Later still, another mother asked me how I managed to "do it." Because "it was so dirty" she had never broached the subject with her own daughter. I think that it is a mistake to suggest that bodily functions are "dirty."

This experience also suggests that it is best to phrase things so that you get responses you can live with. In other words, don't ask a child if he or she wants a bath/shower. Ask instead, "Do you want a bubble bath or a plain bath?" "Do you want to compete, or sit and cheer for your teammates?"

ADJUSTMENTS

When Elaine was very young she had hearing aids. She has had glasses from the time she was six months old. The challenge was how to fit the hearing aids and glasses around her tiny ears. A wonderful optician helped us alter the glasses so that the hearing aids went around the ear and the glasses were altered so they stopped short of the ear and a tiny hole was punched into it. The ends of an elastic band went through one of the holes, and we could loosen or tighten the elastic as needed so that the glasses sat comfortably and firmly on her head. The hearing aids went around each ear but were also secured to the elastic band holding the glasses on her head. It worked.

Elaine has a good sense of what to wear for each of her jobs and several of her activities. She takes care of her clothes and generally looks well put together. The challenge comes in finding clothing that works for her. Elaine is short and round. Typically, if it is a good fit around her middle, the hem or pant legs are too long. I hem lots of her clothes. She doesn't do well with V-necks as the V plunges too low for her body. She doesn't like scratchy clothes or turtlenecks. Pull-on pants work better than those with buttons and zippers, and she tends to pull shirts with buttons over her head when she dresses or undresses. Her counselor and I support her by doing a survey of her clothing at the beginning of each season. Clothes that are too tight or too worn are removed from her closet and either tossed or given away.

COMMUNITY

Some members of my family were shocked that I did not put Elaine's name on a waiting list for a segregated "ranch" in a southern state that provides jobs, housing, and social activities for people with Down syndrome within the grounds of the property. And later, when I was facing two surgeries in less than two months, my family advocated putting her on a waiting list for a group home. They believed that moving my daughter into a setting where others "took care of" things was the answer. While they would never want their own children or grandchildren to be isolated in such a segregated setting, they don't see segregation as the issue—they see long-term supervision and monitoring as the issue. If not an agency, then who will be there for Elaine when I am gone?

Some would argue that individuals in a setting like a ranch or group home are part of a community – and it certainly is true for many, but it is often the case that once the parental supervision is gone, the situation changes. Ranches may seem like retirement communities, but without careful supervision, the potential for segregation from the broader community is huge. Often folks with developmental disabilities are not particularly articulate about their needs and that is, of course, one dimension to the problem. Another is that agencies are overly concerned about safety—a good thing to a point, but "safety" concerns can be used to justify isolation. With group homes, staffing issues often dictate that everyone in the group home goes to an activity, or no one goes. A group home for my daughter, at this point in her life, would be a huge step backwards. She is incredibly involved in the community, and is out and about most evenings.

WHY WOULD ANYONE WISH TO CURTAIL THAT?

Although I have a special-needs trust for her, and have joined an organization that will provide input to the trustees on how Elaine is doing with her jobs and in her home once I am gone, the real answer to what happens when I die is the intentional community created for her.

Currently, I am working to expand this intentional community The intentional community provides the supports and collectively provides the supervision to ensure that Elaine's needs and desires are considered. People in that community have different roles, and some are paid while others are not paid. They communicate with each other periodically and are tuned into Elaine. When I am no longer able to perform my role as parent and advocate, members of her community or "team" can assume different aspects of the role I play in Elaine's life. And, when a member of her team moves away or is no longer able to support Elaine in any way, the others in her intentional community will know enough about Elaine to help her find a replacement.

Elaine is part of many communities, but most of those groups have a unique and special focus. They really are not designed to support an individual in the way an intentional community is. So the key to continuity and richness in Elaine's life after I am gone is an intentional community.

Currently, I am one of the founding members of a nonprofit created to support adults with developmental disabilities as they move into their own places in the community. Integrated Living Opportunities (ILO) is committed to building the infrastructure that will support and sustain these intentional communities. The goal is to create intentional communities that provide the support that ensures individuals are able to be full participants in their community so they can live with dignity and fulfill their dreams. At my age there is a real urgency to make this work.

The first step to creating a community for Elaine in her new place involved identifying the community of paid and unpaid supports she already had. Before she moved out of the family home, she was an active participant in several groups, and many members of these groups were already part of Elaine's community. When she moved out, we needed to add people to her community. We want her to maintain the friendships she already has and to develop new ones. Of particular interest is the desire to develop friendships in her new neighborhood.

How do you build a community? In the example of the playgroup, there was a purpose for getting together on a regular basis. The children got to know each other and so did the parents. The children got to know the parents of their friends. That is what made it possible for parents in the playgroup to help me when we were robbed and when Louis seriously injured himself in a fall. My children knew the parents of their playgroup friends and were not afraid to go with them.

In the case of church, it took participation in services and, in the early days, Sunday school. Unique events, expand and extend those connections. The support we received following Elaine's surgery is an example of how relationships deepened at our church.

In Special Olympics, each sport team works hard to develop a sense of community during their season. What makes bowling particularly successful in building a community is, in part, the nature of the sport: athletes sit in the lane waiting for their turn. This gives athletes opportunities to talk and cheer for each other. For bowling, there is also a weekly newsletter that disseminates information about upcoming events and highlights achievements of the athletes. All this helps build a sense of community.

• •

The intentional community I am working to create for my daughter—as well as for me, as I age—involves building connections. The idea is for everyone in Elaine's community to be comfortable with each other and to have an understanding of how they each support Elaine. No single individual knows how to do it all, but collectively they have the knowledge to help Elaine navigate the various agencies and organizations that support her and identify when new ones are needed.

LOW FUNCTIONING OR FEW SKILLS?

Too many people describe folks with developmental delays in terms of "functioning." "Oh," people say, "your daughter must be high functioning because she lives in her own place." The answer is, not really. She just keeps learning new skills. Hence, I prefer to describe her in terms of the skills she has acquired. Skills can be learned and practiced. Using the term "functioning" to describe someone's abilities implies limits.

When she was very little, a therapist told me that the more I did with Elaine, the more she would be able to do. How very true that advice was!

At thirty, Elaine moved into her own place. This capped years of preparation. Nothing trumps baby steps, practice, and more baby steps. Elaine began by being responsible for her own laundry and room. Then she began baking her own bread when she was diagnosed with Celiac Sprue and could not eat gluten. She learned to use a boxed gluten-free bread mix and a bread machine. It took time, but making bread every eight to nine days meant she had plenty of practice.

In her teens she began vacuuming the house. It turns out she *loves* bagless machines (where she can see the dirt swirl around), and anyone even thinking of using the vacuum has to duke it out with her.

Next, we introduced her to cleaning the bathroom she shared with her brother. It turned out that the critical piece for Elaine was color coordination. Pink was the color. We found a pink double bucket (water in one side, "stuff" in the other), pink rubber gloves (I can't remember how we found those), and pink toilet brush. Elaine doesn't use Clorox, ammonia, or other caustic chemicals, and I had the kind of prefab showers and tubs that can't take them anyway. Windex is used liberally (and no doubt not efficiently). Sometimes she uses vinegar and baking soda, but mostly she uses soap, elbow grease, and Windex.

Next she began to work on the wooden floors. There is a special product we use on them. Needless to say it is *liberally* applied by Elaine when she tends to the floors. So we go through supplies, but everything looks good and is somewhat clean once she is finished. The important thing is she is responsible for it, takes pride in it, and appears to initiate cleaning when she feels it is needed (happily about once a week) I miss this help now that she is in her own place!

Elaine began preparing her own meals (and often cooked for me as well) in her early twenties. She doesn't use either the oven or stove by herself, so sometimes she works with her counselor. But on her own she can use a soup maker, a blender, a George Foreman grill, a sandwich grill (don't ask . . . I have no idea who gave that to her—it has no ridges, the George Foreman does), a toaster, the microwave, and an electric kettle.

Elaine's nutritional sensibilities took hold simply because she began to bring home fresh vegetables from one of her jobs and she was motivated to eat them. She would arrive home thrilled with her bags of vegetables and state that we needed to cook them. Since she won't eat fruits and vegetables raw, she tried various recipes for cooking them. Her preference was for squash soup and lettuce soup, and she loved making pesto for her gluten-free pasta. She kept the recipes she liked, and several years ago those became the basis of a cookbook she gave as gifts. The lesson here is that planting, weeding, and harvesting vegetables have a positive impact on one's diet.

She reads food labels for information regarding gluten, but she doesn't necessarily pay attention to anything else, nor is she really astute about expiration dates. Smell and looks dictate to her when to toss food out.

While still at home she was responsible for emptying trash into appropriate receptacles, hauling it out to the corner, and then bringing the empties back. It was her job—even when she wasn't always enthusiastic about it.

The point of all this is, Elaine has significant developmental delays. The skills she has learned were introduced over time, and she has had opportunities to practice them. No tricks to it at all. Baby steps, practice, and then the next baby step. What motivated Elaine? She likes being able to say "my job to do" and "I am independent." But let's be frank; hunger works really, really well, and before I retired, I didn't always get home in time to fix dinner when she was hungry, so out of necessity (and knowing how to manipulate her appliances), she got it together. When she moved into her own place, I lost a cook, a cleaner, and a weeder!

What amazes me is the number of parents who wait until their child is ready to leave school before they begin to teach them life skills. Learning these skills and having opportunities to practice them over time works.

MOVING INTO A PLACE OF ONE'S OWN

Elaine was ready to move when she was twenty-six, because that is when *she* wanted to move out. I assumed that we would wait for a housing voucher—but then after years of waiting, she got a voucher! —That is when I realized that moving her out of the family home involved more than bricks and mortar. The voucher was for a studio apartment about twenty-five miles away from our home. She would have been far away from her jobs, the community she knew, and from any support in an emergency. Community took on a new meaning. We did not accept the voucher.

A year before Elaine moved into her own place, I attended a presentation by The Center for Independent Futures® (CIF), an organization in Evanston, Illinois. After that meeting, the woman who hosted the workshop, arranged a trip to Evanston for the five families interested in learning more about CIF. Although I was somewhat skeptical, once I saw CIF's office and visited the various residences of the participants, I was convinced that the model created by CIF was possible and, more importantly, sustainable. When I returned home, I got motivated. Under the leadership of the wise woman who found CIF and brought them to the D.C. area for that workshop, a non-profit, Integrated Living Opportunities (ILO) was created. Then the families who established ILO explored residential options. It became clear to me that renting presented as many challenges as purchasing a place for my daughter. I then found a real estate agent and began looking for inexpensive and affordable condos. I found one, and learned that Fanny Mae had a way for me to purchase the unit as if I were moving in. This meant financing the mortgage was cheaper. The condo was too close to my home to have been considered a second home; otherwise it would be considered an investment. However, a parent can, under Fanny Mae, purchase a unit for a disabled dependent. This made the purchase of a condo for Elaine affordable.

Elaine moved in to the condo on October 26, 2014. I use Craigslist to find roommates. Both her first roommate and her second have been neurotypical young women close in age to Elaine. The roommate is an overnight presence, and far more importantly, she is expected to get Elaine off to work on time in the morning—or call the job coach to let her know when Elaine left if she won't be on time. The condo is a two bedroom with each bedroom having its own full bath and walk-in closet. The transition from my home to the condo was relatively smooth. In short order Elaine referred to the condo as her home as the other one as "Mom's house."

Since moving in, Elaine has been supported in the morning with a "wake up" check by her roommate, and during the week she has a counselor, or personal support who is with her in the late afternoon and evening. When her personal support leaves in the evening, electronics are off and Elaine is headed to bed. After problems with nodding off at work on Monday mornings, we added a Sunday night check to ensure Elaine headed to bed at a reasonable hour. Initially I called in the mornings just before she was scheduled to leave to wish her a good day. It took a while, but she almost always answered the phone and said she was getting ready to leave.

OUT AND ABOUT IN THE COMMUNITY

Elaine is familiar with her neighborhood. She knows her way around and she is recognized at the shops and library where she goes frequently. The cashiers at the grocery store ask about her when I shop alone. Her familiarity with her surroundings and the fact that people in the community recognize her helps create a safe environment for her. Whenever she begins something new, perhaps a winter art class after work in another suburban community, her job coach reviews the route with her and then shadows her to ensure she arrives safely. Once the routine is established, Elaine is able to follow it.

When she first moved out, I went to the local police station to see if there was anything I should do to indicate to them that an individual with a developmental disability was living in a particular condominium complex. We live in a suburban community in a large county. There are lots of different police officers on various shifts. There is no practical way to introduce my daughter to all of them. The officers at our local district office told me that there were devices for individuals who were "runners," and the county's emergency call-in center had a system for identifying people who called frequently, but nothing specific for someone like Elaine. We have an emergency plan that includes what to do in various types of emergencies and that, plus building on her skills and developing new ones, will have to suffice. Emergency scenarios are reviewed and appropriate responses to them are rehearsed as needed.

One afternoon, Elaine locked herself out of her condo when she stepped outside and the door swung closed behind her. She had no key, no phone, but she was with her counselor who had a key. This was a teachable moment. When she first moved in, we attempted to build a relationship with neighbors on her landing. We had some success with an elderly woman across the landing, but she moved months after Elaine moved in. Her high school friend lives about two blocks away, but with no phone, Elaine would not be able to call her, and walking over would not necessarily solve the problem if her friend was out. The solution to this problem was a combination lock. There still is a key that can be used, but a combination will unlock the door.

Burnt toast is a phenomenon many of us have experienced. We had to teach Elaine to unplug the toaster and turn it upside down in the sink—burnt toast and all the crumbs. Her first impulse was to put the toast in the trash, but there is always the possibility that a cinder might spark a fire. There is also a fire extinguisher that is easy for her to operate under her sink. Its use is practiced on a routine basis.

Elaine often is late for work because when she gets to the transit center to transfer from one bus to another, she will stop and talk to Jehovah's Witnesses and others who hand out flyers and pamphlets. This is worrying, but even when we put a stop to it temporarily, we don't eliminate this practice. Occasionally, she will strike up a conversation with someone on the bus, but generally she sits quietly. I have shadowed her at times and noticed that if anyone starts to talk loudly or seems to be looking at her, she moves her seat closer to the driver. She has an awareness of what is going on around her.

When I first retired and Elaine was still living at home, I became anxious one afternoon when she had not returned from work a good two hours after I expected her. I contacted her job coach who assured me Elaine had left on time and knew her bus routes. Another hour passed, and just as I was thinking of whom to contact, I saw her. She was singing and walking along the sidewalk totally unaware of the late hour. Apparently, she had fallen asleep, and as short as she is, slumped over in her seat at the back of the bus, she went unnoticed. She had slept through at least two round trips before she woke up, refreshed, and got off at her stop.

As to buses and travel training, Elaine is short; the traffic is heavy on the bus route near our home, so Elaine got on and off the bus at the same stop. She did not cross the highway. It made her commute to work longer, but it was safer. Moving to her condo placed her within four blocks of the transit center and it shortens her daily commute considerably. As her bus to the transit center is on a side street, she uses the crosswalk and gets on and off the bus on different sides of the road.

In the past two years Elaine has picked up some bad habits while waiting for buses at the bus transit center. To prevent her from hunting through trash cans for food, she now takes taxis to and from work.

. . . .

TRAVEL

Elaine flew on a plane by herself for the first time at the age of thirty-one. She has frequent-flyer miles, earned from years of visiting her father who lived in the middle of the country, but at that time she always traveled with her brother. This first solo flight was a big step that demonstrated her independence and boosted her confidence. I accompanied her to the gate and her stepmother met her at the other end, but in Elaine's mind she did it all by herself.

Was I nervous? Not really. I have flown with Elaine and knew that she could handle the TSA procedures. Once when we were leaving Denver, I was stopped and pulled behind a curtained off area for additional screening. Elaine had already made it through the TSA lines and it was possible she would leave the area. Denver has a "train" that carries passengers to various terminals. I could not see Elaine, my purse, or my suitcase. When I was cleared, I was relieved to see Elaine sitting on the suitcases with my purse in her hand. She knew the procedures and wasn't at all anxious. She just asked if I was OK, because, "I am here, Mom."

MANAGING A LIFE

Besides the notebook that held a summary of therapist and doctor visits, I kept and still keep a calendar of important dates in Elaine's life: reminders of when medications need to be refilled, regular checkups scheduled, paratransit identification renewed, the expiration date for her state ID, etc. In the early days, I was Elaine's unpaid and unofficial case manager. As Elaine matured, I maintained records but stepped back so she could manage more of her own life. Early on, with Elaine's consent, I got durable power of attorney, as well as financial- and medical-agent status. I chose not to become her guardian.

In my state, guardianship essentially makes my daughter a ward of the court. True, I would be her court-appointed guardian, but only at the court's pleasure. In our area of the world, courts have not always been kind to parents who wish to relinquish guardianship so that their child can be independent. Nor is it unheard of for the court to shift guardianship from a parent to an agency. For these reasons I did not choose to be a guardian. Instead I have a series of documents that, with Elaine's consent, empower me to act on her behalf.

THE SANDWICH GENERATION

By my late fifties, my mother was a widow and lived nearby in an independent living situation. She spent enough time at our home that the guest room was dubbed "Grandma's Room." We went to church on Sundays and had adventures before returning home. I checked with her before the holidays to ensure she had plans; if not, she generally joined us. When she needed assistance, but didn't want to move into assisted living, I stepped up my involvement in her life. At the time, my children were transitioning from middle to high school. Between the demands of my job, my children, and my mother, time was often in short supply.

Then, suddenly, my mother died. Shortly after her death, members of my church asked me to seriously consider joining a caregivers support group. It was a great group and I was glad to join. However, I was startled to learn I had been invited because I was seen as the caregiver for my daughter. In my mind, my role as caregiver was with my mother; I was just parenting my daughter. It certainly proves that we often do not see ourselves as others see us!

Personally, I never liked it when people told me I was blessed to have a child with a disability. I don't imagine anyone wishes their child had a disability. I also never liked it when my mother praised me for all I did with Elaine. I wish she had praised me for keeping calm and having a sense of humor, anything but praising me for helping Elaine get the services she needed. That praise seemed to imply that I considered doing nothing. Doing nothing was never an option. Holding it together and not acting on my emotions was an effort at times. It is that effort that deserves praise.

A FULL LIFE

Elaine has jobs Monday through Friday and events most weekday evenings. Between Special Olympics, the gym, a PCR conversation class, the integrated percussion band, and her social events, Elaine has a full life. The Center for Independent Futures® has a graphic that is a visual representation of a full life. In the center is a circle (dreams and goals) and eight circles surround it representing all aspects of a full life: the spiritual, friends, health, lifelong learning, etc.) Elaine's circles are full of activities and people. Her intentional community assists her in realizing her dreams and achieving her goals.

However, let it be said that Elaine is not like some of her friends who were more successful academically in school. They get together frequently to hang out and are adept on their iPhones. Elaine is just learning to work with her cell phone and her interaction with friends tends to be at the events and activities she attends. Yet, her life is full and it works for her.

Elaine takes her responsibilities as a citizen seriously. She recycles. She uses the crosswalk. She votes. When she receives the League of Women Voters information on candidates running for office, she sits with me as I read the information to her. She then takes the sample ballot that accompanies the League's information and she marks her votes. She takes the sample ballot to the polling booth on Election Day. One of her stepsisters was surprised when Elaine asked her which presidential candidate she preferred. The stepsister said she never thought she would have a discussion about candidates with Elaine. Elaine's choices reflect her understanding of which candidate will best serve her. Isn't that what many of us do?

When she moved into her own place, she just changed her residence and moved closer to the "action" in our suburban neighborhood. She already had a "life." Now she is within walking distance of movies, restaurants, shops, the library, and an arts center. She is also closer to the transit center and the express bus that links our neighborhood to the Washington Metro. Right now she is living the life she wants and is using the skills she has worked on for years.

Louis landed a full-time job in December 2014. He has social activities and friends. He is living the life he wants. At the time he was still living at home. He moved into his own place in 2019. Louis has a condo about a mile from Elaine. The morning after his move, Louis told me it was wonderful being on his own.

I started to travel internationally when I retired in 2011. Elaine handles my absences well, in part because I send daily emails to her counselor who shares them with her. Once she called me on my cell phone to let me know she missed me and it was time for me to come home. My flight home was scheduled for the next day, so I don't really know if she believes my return home was a result of her call, but I know twenty-one days away is probably long enough for both of us.

A friend told me, "You're not butter, so don't spread yourself so thin!" I do try to focus my energy, but it is certainly true that I am busier in retirement than I ever imagined I would be. Besides being a parent and managing my own household, I also was Elaine's support broker. Basically that means we shifted from an agency to a self-directed waiver. Elaine is the employer and although I served as her support broker for years, now a friend with years of budget experience helps her supervise her employees and manage their timesheets and the DDA funds that make up her budget.

Another important role for me involved the nonprofit created in 2014 to support Elaine and others like her as they move into their own places in the community. I was a founding member and was on the board of Integrated Living Opportunities. I also administered the skills inventory for the organization. The skills inventory identifies the current skill level of young adults with developmental disabilities and identifies activities that will develop or maintain the skills they will need as they transition from their parents' home to their own place in the community. The idea is to help Elaine—and others like her—maintain their skills and develop new ones. The goal is to provide the necessary supports so that each can be as in control of his or her life as possible. Safety is important, but not at the expense of the ability to live one's life as fully as possible.

A MATTER OF PERSPECTIVE

When my children were born, I was a month shy of my thirty-ninth birthday. The fact that I would be in my retirement years when they were approaching thirty meant it was important to figure out what Elaine needed to learn, and to start teaching her early so that she would not be dependent on me as an adult. Not every family has that perspective. I remember a conversation with a mother in St. Louis. Her daughter was twelve. Elaine was six when I shared my hope that Elaine would be able to live on her own in the community. The mother was shocked, telling me that she would never even consider doing that. I have lost touch with that family, so I don't know where her daughter is now, but Elaine is living in her own place in the community. She is pleased with her life. So are we. It represents a huge achievement, but it is still a work in progress.

Because doctors told me at her two-week checkup that she would stop learning at the age of seven, I tried to figure out what we needed to do and how we should do it. Whenever I saw a child with Down syndrome older than Elaine, I always asked the parent for advice. I asked what they thought had helped their child acquire so many skills at such a young age. One mother told me that she had been given a choice of focusing on academic skills or social skills and decided social skills were the most important initially. That made sense to me, and while we still worked on the skills that would lead to letter recognition and simple math, we focused on social behaviors and other social skills.

Once she was in preschool and then public schools, having Elaine included in classes with non-disabled classmates gave her lots of role models that helped her learn social norms as well as language skills. It also meant that she had friends in the neighborhood.

By the time Elaine turned twenty-one and ended her time in public education, she was able to read words and count to one hundred. Before she turned thirty, she could read simple sentences, do simple arithmetic, and engage in articulate conversations. Clearly she did not stop learning at age seven! More importantly, by the time she moved into her own place, she had mastered basic independent living skills and learned how to get to and from her jobs on public transportation.

Safety is always a concern. Her job coach shadows her periodically to ensure she is crossing streets safely and watching traffic as she travels on public transportation. There have been times when she has shared her private information with strangers, and her brother has talked about bringing her back home to live. We have not done so, choosing instead to help her to understand the importance of keeping her information private, and shadowing her as she travels independently. The dilemma is how to balance safety with her right to live her life as independently as possible.

Elaine, with her special needs is not so different from my mother when she began to need support in her old age. We wanted my mother to be safe, but mother was fierce in her desire to remain as much in control of her life as possible. Safety is something everyone understands. Autonomy is something we tend to understand best when our own is threatened. Not everyone understands the importance of autonomy for Elaine. The type of community I hope to build for Elaine is not so different from what I hope to have supporting me as I begin to experience the challenges of old age. In other words I want for both Elaine and for me a community that will allow each of us to live the lives we want while minimizing risks. What does that mean? It means having the right to plan our activities, have privacy, and make choices about what and when we want to eat and where we want to live.

· ·

I am retired. For a while I remained in the family home, but I recognized that my children would not be able to care for me as I aged. I sold my house, helped my son find his own place, and moved into a nearby continuing care community. It was a good decision and a great move. I am living a full life, and have not slowed down in the least. Downsizing from a four-bedroom home to a one-bedroom apartment was a challenge, but my son was able to furnish his condo and other family members enjoyed selecting pieces to take for their homes. Neighbors took garden tools and finally the Salvation Army got it's turn. It wasn't easy, but was not quite as traumatic as I imagined it might be. In the end I still moved with too much "stuff" and need to continue to downsize from my new place. I am living a full life and see no reason to slow down, but I know my days of slowing down and more downsizing is coming. When it does, I hope I have as many choices as I have created for my daughter.

In the late 1990s, I began managing a ten-pin bowling program for our local Special Olympics. I no longer manage the program that starts in late August and ends in May with a short break in the winter months. I recruited a team to replace me and run the program. The Covid pandemic took its toll on the Special Olympic sailing program that at one point involved my Monday evening and weekends during the summer. I remain active in church and use the time after church to explore the many opportunities the Washington, DC metropolitan area has to offer. I also travel both within the United States and internationally.

I continue to support my daughter. I have a large loose leave notebook with everything about Elaine from her daily schedule, her medical issues, to when she signs up for various activities, when her various documents need to be renewed, addresses, and contact information for her friends and so on. I keep the notebook up to date. I also regularly review her legal documents with my attorney every 5 years to ensure everything is in order.

No one can know the future, but I have tried to plan for it. In late 2020 I was diagnosed with Parkinson's Disease. The best prescription is exercise and I exercise daily. So far I have been able to keep the progression of Parkinson's at bay.

Elaine has Down syndrome which means she has three copies of the 21st chromosome. The Alzheimer's gene is on the 21st chromosome. She has three copies of the gene, so it is likely Alzheimer's is in her future.

Meanwhile, we enjoy visiting museums and gardens on weekends and planning our next trip. Louis is far more independent, but joins us for holiday dinners and always responds to Elaine's requests for help.

Our lives have been full. We have had challenges. We have had many joys and so very many blessings.

www.ingramcontent.com/pod-product-compliance
Lightning Source LLC
LaVergne TN
LVHW041641060526
838200LV00040B/1663